Weathering the Storm: Canadian-U.S. Relations, 1980–83

by David Leyton-Brown

Canadian-American Committee

Sponsored by
■ C.D. Howe Institute (Canada)
■ National Planning Association (U.S.A.)

327.71
L685w

Canadian Cataloguing in Publication Data

Leyton-Brown, David, 1946–
    Weathering the storm: Canadian-U.S. relations, 1980–83

"CAC 51"
Includes bibliographical references.
ISBN 0-88806-127-7

1. Canada — Relations — United States.
2. United States — Relations — Canada.
I. Canadian-American Committee. II. Title.

FC 249.L49 1985   327.71073   C85-098176-X
F1029.5.U6L49 1985

85-5139

Quotation with appropriate credit is permissible.
C.D. Howe Institute (Toronto, Ontario) and
National Planning Association (Washington, D.C.)

Printed in Canada — March 1985.
Can.$8.00, U.S.$6.50

Contents

A Statement by the Canadian-American Committee to Accompany the Report on

Weathering the Storm: Canadian-U.S. Relations, 1980–83

In 1981 the Canadian-American Committee published *Improving Bilateral Consultation on Economic Issues: A Policy Statement*, in which it expressed its concern about the tendencies of the governments of both Canada and the United States to take unilateral initiatives without regard to bilateral consequences. Such tendencies have become sources of tensions in the relationship. This was certainly the case at the beginning of the 1980s.

The Committee recognizes that a complex interplay of domestic interests, formal arrangements, and informal expectations shapes Canadian-U.S. relations. To further an understanding of how tensions have been managed in the early 1980s, the Committee has sponsored *Weathering the Storm: Canadian-U.S. Relations, 1980–83*. It presents case studies of three key bilateral incidents of the 1980–83 period — the introduction of Canada's National Energy Program (NEP), the United States' consideration of a private-sector petition to impose countervailing duties on imports of softwood lumber from Canada, and the ongoing dispute over Canada's restrictions on televised advertising aimed at Canadian audiences and broadcast from U.S. border stations. It is hoped that the lessons drawn from these recent disputes will contribute to more effective management of the inevitable stresses that will arise in future.

The potential agenda of issues is fluid and unpredictable because the two countries are so interdependent and because both have a wide range of domestic interests with a stake in bilateral trade and investment. If the management of the agenda is to be more predictable in future, decision-makers, in both the public and private sectors, must become more aware of the longer-term mutual benefits that accrue from a cooperative relationship. Because each country's vulnerability to unilateral protective action by the other is increasing, the costs will be high if a pattern of national action, reaction, and retaliation becomes established.[1]

One lesson of the 1980–83 experience is that multilateral commitments and dispute-settlement mechanisms can provide an effective means of resolving bilateral problems. For example, U.S. complaints about domestic-

---

[1] Each dispute adds fuel to, and alters the viewpoints of participants in, other trade-related arguments. The cumulative damage of just the three tense situations described in this paper will take some years of trust and cooperation to repair. — **Ray V. Smith**

procurement regulations proposed under the NEP and required by Canada's *Foreign Investment Review Act* were dealt with to the satisfaction of both countries by reference to obligations and procedures under the General Agreement on Tariffs and Trade (GATT).

Some issues, such as trade in services, have very limited coverage under multilateral agreements. The dispute over border broadcasting indicates that tensions are likely to persist in the absence of mutually accepted standards. Other issues, such as the national treatment of investment, are subject only to statements of principle, which may be interpreted very differently by each country.[2]

Bilateral agreements also need strengthening and extension into new areas. For example, in the Committee's view, both countries would benefit from reinforcing an open world trade and payments system. In conjunction with efforts to strengthen the multilateral system, the two countries could cooperate bilaterally in pioneering some of the processes and initiatives necessary to help sustain economic growth through the international exchange of goods and services.

Although strengthening formal bilateral and multilateral arrangements can avoid some problems and help in the resolution of others, strains will still arise. Managing these tensions will require patient and diligent efforts by Canadian and U.S. decisionmakers. The postwar period of quiet diplomacy and special relationship ended some years ago. Both countries have changed greatly, and other countries clamor for a special relationship with the United States.

The Committee believes that careful and objective analysis of recent bilateral issues will contribute to informed public debate and help put the relationship on firmer footing. The author of this study, Dr. David Leyton-Brown, an associate professor at York University in Toronto, has been an independent analyst and commentator on Canadian-U.S. relations for more than a decade. While all aspects and findings of this study do not necessarily represent the views of any individual member, the Committee as a whole endorses its publication.

In particular, the Committee endorses the author's recommendation that both countries should develop a framework of understanding that embodies broad principles for guiding the future conduct of Canadian-U.S. relations.

---

[2] Moreover, issues concerning investment, even in the absence of particular discrimination against foreign companies, can exacerbate bilateral tensions when there are asymmetries in the policies of the two countries. An example of this is in the area of intellectual property rights, a necessary condition for a positive environment for investment, especially in the research-based, high-technology sectors. In the United States, for example, full patent protection exists for all products, while in Canada, patent protection for pharmaceuticals and foods does not. Through a compulsory licensing provision in Canadian law, these products are excluded from full patent protection in Canada, and the effect of this difference has been an exacerbation of tension between the two countries. — **Thomas J. Connors**

Basic points that should be considered include:

* *Understanding the motives and priorities of the other government.* The potential for misunderstanding can be reduced by encouraging greater continuity of contact among legislators, cabinet members, government officials, and private-sector leaders.
* *Choosing policy instruments that will achieve the desired objective while minimizing the costs imposed on the other country.* Many problems can be avoided if policy design in each country includes consideration of the possible consequences for the other and a willingness to seek alternatives that minimize adverse consequences.
* *Developing a fuller process of consultation.* Effective consultation can promote better understanding, ensure early warning of adverse consequences resulting from the actions of the other government, help prevent inadvertent injury to the other country, and offer opportunities for conciliation and the design of more mutually beneficial policy alternatives.
* *Avoiding the linkage of unrelated issues as a coercive tactic.* Both countries should seek to resolve problems expeditiously and avoid linking issues in a manner that threatens an escalating cycle of retaliation and reaction.[3]

The application of these principles — which build from the position taken by the Committee in its 1981 Statement recommending a bilateral consultative mechanism — would help Canada and the United States to work together more effectively in the application of their formal obligations to the conduct of bilateral issues and assist in the resolution of problems that are not subject to such arrangements.

No one can doubt that this important bilateral economic relationship requires special care and attention. In an ever more complex and interdependent world, Canada and the United States have an enduring interest in resolving bilateral issues and developing common approaches to global economic relations. With political renewal in both countries, this is a particularly opportune time to build on recent experience and to explore new approaches to the challenges of interdependence.

---

[3] An additional basic point would be: recognizing asymmetries in investment conditions, which can lead to bilateral tensions and which can be a source of nontariff trade barriers. — **Thomas J. Connors**

Members of the Canadian-American Committee Signing the Statement

Cochairmen

STEPHEN C. EYRE
Citicorp Professor of Finance, Pace University

ADAM H. ZIMMERMAN
President and Chief Operating Officer, Noranda Inc.

Vice Chairmen

WILLIAM D. EBERLE
Chairman, EBCO Incorporated

J.H. WARREN
Vice Chairman, Bank of Montreal

Members

EDWIN L. ARTZT
President, Procter & Gamble International and Vice Chairman of the Procter & Gamble Company

CHARLES F. BAIRD
Chairman and Chief Executive Officer, INCO Limited

RALPH M. BARFORD
President, Valleydene Corporation Ltd.

R.R. BAXTER
President, CF Industries

ROD J. BILODEAU
Chairman and Chief Executive Officer, Honeywell Limited

DAVID I.W. BRAIDE
Vice-Chairman, C-I-L Inc.

PHILIP BRIGGS
Executive Vice-President, Metropolitan Life Insurance Company

KENNETH J. BROWN
President, Graphic Communication International Union

LAWRENCE BURKHART
President, Canadian Kenworth

JOE E. CHENOWETH
Executive Vice-President, International Controls, Honeywell Inc.

W.A. COCHRANE
Chairman and Chief Executive Officer, Connaught Laboratories Limited

*THOMAS J. CONNORS
Executive Vice-President, Operations, Pfizer International Inc.

CHARLES E. CRAIG
Vice-President, International Operations, The Timken Company

PETER DeMAY
Group Vice-President, Fluor Engineers Inc.

JOHN H. DICKEY, Q.C.
President, Nova Scotia Pulp Limited

WILLIAM DIEBOLD, JR.
Upper Nyack, New York

THOMAS W. diZEREGA
Upperville, Virginia

RODNEY S.C. DONALD
Chairman, McLean Budden Limited

CHARLES F. DORAN
Professor and Director, Center of Canadian Studies, Johns Hopkins University School of Advanced International Studies

JOHN P. FISHER
Chairman, Fraser Inc.

ROY A. GENTLES
President and Chief Executive Officer, Alcan Aluminum Corporation

JAMES K. GRAY
Executive Vice-President, Canadian Hunter Exploration, Ltd.

JOHN A. HANNAH
President Emeritus, Michigan State University

WILLIAM R. HARRIS
Senior Vice-President, International, PPG Industries, Inc.

JOHN B. HASELTINE
Senior Vice-President, The First National Bank of Chicago

J. PAUL HELLSTROM
Managing Director, The First Boston Corporation

STANDLEY H. HOCH
Vice-President and Treasurer, General Electric Company

E. SYDNEY JACKSON
President, The Manufacturers Life Insurance Company

*See footnotes to the Statement.

---

*See footnotes to the Statement.

R.D. WENDEBORN
Executive Vice-President, Ingersoll-Rand Company

P.N.T. WIDDRINGTON
President and Chief Executive Officer, John Labatt
Limited

WILLIAM P. WILDER
Chairman of the Board, The Consumers' Gas Company
Ltd.

LYNTON R. WILSON
President and Chief Executive Officer, Redpath Industries
Limited

FRANCIS G. WINSPEAR
Edmonton, Alberta

GEORGE W. WOODS
Vice-Chairman, TransCanada PipeLines Limited

CHARLES WOOTTON
Director, International Public Affairs, Gulf Oil
Corporation

J.O. WRIGHT
Secretary, Canadian Co-Operative Wheat Producers
Limited

HAL E. WYATT
Vice-Chairman, The Royal Bank of Canada

Weathering the Storm:
Canadian-U.S. Relations,
1980–83

Acknowledgements

This study would not have been possible without the frank cooperation of many present and former officials of both governments in providing information about the cases in question, and in responding to earlier drafts of the manuscript. I am grateful to them and to members of the private sector who provided similar invaluable assistance.

I am also grateful to Rod Byers and the staff of the York University Research Programme in Strategic Studies, who provided a working environment in which I could carry out my research and writing. My research assistant, Howard Silverman, showed particular initiative and effort.

Finally, I wish to express my appreciation to my wife, Anne, and my children, Kevin and Allison, whose family life was disrupted more than they expected by my labors, but who provided me with the support and encouragement I needed.

David Leyton-Brown
Toronto, 1985

1

Introduction

The relationship between Canada and the United States is often turbulent and occasionally stormy. From 1980 through 1983, tensions increased dramatically and then eased. Such fluctuations in the tone and conduct of the relationship are understandable because, despite their common continent and heritage, the two countries differ considerably in structure, tradition, policy goals, and the methods chosen to reach those goals. These differences have contributed to disputes between them and can be expected to do so in future. Increasing interdependence, however, means that each country has an ever-larger stake in resolving the differences.

The inextricable economic relationship that now exists between Canada and the United States is clearly evident in their trade and investment patterns. They share the world's largest volume of bilateral trade, valued at U.S.$98 billion in 1983. Canada is the United States' most important trading partner: its 20 percent share of U.S. exports in 1983 was double that of Japan and greater than that of the ten-nation European Community. But the trading relationship also reflects the economic asymmetry of the two countries. Trade has always meant more to Canada than to the United States because it is such an important factor in its national income — 28 percent of Canada's GNP is accounted for by exports. Seventy percent of those exports go to the United States. In contrast, the United States depends on exports for only 10 percent of its GNP.

Each country is also the other's largest foreign investor, but again, the relationship is asymmetrical. As of 1982, for example, U.S. direct investment in Canada exceeded a total of U.S.$46 billion, while Canada's direct investment in the United States amounted to more than U.S.$18 billion.[1] Although the value of U.S. direct investment in Canada is more than double Canadian direct investment in the United States, the Canadian investment stake in the United States has been growing more rapidly and is relatively much larger on a per capita basis.

---

[1] The source for U.S. direct investment in Canada is R. Scholl, "The International Investment Position of the United States," *Survey of Current Business* 64 (June 1984): 74–78. The source for Canadian direct investment in the United States is Statistics Canada, *Statistics Canada Daily*, Cat. no. 11–001, April 27, 1984, pp. 7–10. Note that investment data are based on the book value and not the replacement value of investment.

Despite the similarities between the two countries and despite the intimacy that has developed from their extensive business and cultural contacts, the people involved in conducting the relationship must take account of important differences between them in national endowments, political structure, and philosophy. Climate, geography, and population size have forced each country into a different pattern of land use. Each has its own distinctive political tradition. Canada's cabinet system of government contrasts with the U.S. presidential system. The laissez-faire individualism of U.S. culture contrasts with Canada's more conservative emphasis on tradition and the allotment of a larger role to government.

The similarities and differences make for a unique relationship, and it would be surprising if the two countries' interdependence did not result in a list of issues requiring resolution. But specific underlying influences shape the agenda of the relationship and also have some bearing on the ways in which problems are managed. Changes in the international environment, national political philosophies, social and political systems, and differing policy initiatives in the two countries all play a role.

Recent trends in the relationship were set in motion in 1971 when the U.S. government, confronted with balance-of-payments problems, refused to provide special treatment for Canada in the imposition of a temporary import surcharge and the Domestic International Sales Corporation tax legislation was passed. In response, Canada directed its policy initiatives towards reducing an apparent vulnerability to the United States. The resultant strains in the relationship eased in the 1976–78 period as communication between the two countries became more effective.[2]

During the 1980–83 period, tensions rose again to levels not seen since the events of 1971. By the end of the period, however, they had eased off because of improved communications, some moderation of unilateral policy initiatives, and the operation of dispute-settlement mechanisms created by multilateral agreements and domestic legislation. Difficulties remained, nevertheless, particularly over such issues as acid rain and Canadian restrictions on televised advertising beamed from the United States to audiences in Canada. Although concerns over Canada's Foreign Investment Review Agency had eased, some provisions of the National Energy Program (NEP) affecting U.S. investors continued to be irritants. Potential sources of further irritation could well arise in the increasingly turbulent international financial and economic environments in which both countries must operate.[3]

---

[2] For a review of the 1976–78 period, see Canadian–American Committee, *Bilateral Relations in an Uncertain World Context: Canada-U.S. Relations in 1978*, CAC no. 46 (Montreal: C.D. Howe Research Institute; Washington, D.C.: National Planning Association, 1978).

[3] Environmental issues are not included here, because of recent work on acid rain by the Canadian-American Committee (see John E. Carroll, *Acid Rain: An Issue in Canadian-American Relations*, CAC no. 49 [Toronto: C.D. Howe Institute; Washington, D.C.: National Planning Association, 1982]) and on transboundary environmental issues by the C.D. Howe

(continued)

Learning from the 1980–83 Experience

This study seeks to learn from recent disputes and their management, and suggests ways of improving the management of the relationship in future. These suggestions are drawn from case studies of three incidents that occurred in the 1980–83 period. The cases were selected because they illustrate the trade, investment, and cultural dimensions of the relationship, the interaction of underlying factors, and the way in which multilateral and bilateral commitments and domestic legislation shaped the governments' responses to disputes between the two countries.

The first case is that of the NEP, which created issues that dominated the bilateral relationship throughout the period. Introduced on October 28, 1980, the NEP was Canada's response to changes in the international oil market that both countries had experienced in the late 1970s. In part, it reflected a long-standing national concern that Canada own and control more of the activity in key sectors such as petroleum. It was also partly determined by consumer resistance to oil price increases and by federal-provincial conflicts over the distribution of resource revenues — Canada's constitution awards the provinces ownership of petroleum and other natural resources. Diverging philosophical views of the governing parties in the two countries added to the difficulties of dispute resolution.

This case provides an example of the recent multilateral approach to handling trade and investment issues. Canada was willing to alter certain trade-related aspects of the NEP that it recognized were inconsistent with the General Agreement on Tariffs and Trade (GATT). At the heart of the differences between the two governments, however, was the principle of national treatment of foreign investment. One of the U.S. government's main concerns with the NEP was that it not set a discriminatory precedent that could be extended to other Canadian sectors or followed by other governments.

The second case studies the issues raised when the United States considered imposing countervailing duties on its imports of Canadian softwood lumber because of an alleged Canadian export subsidy. The charges of subsidies, which came from some U.S. producers, originated in differences in the commercial and regulatory systems in the lumber industries in the two countries and in the commercial gains these private interests thought they could achieve under the U.S. countervailing duty process. The softwood-lumber case illustrates how a bilateral trade dispute may be treated under the provisions of U.S. trade law, which are in line with the GATT *Agreement on Subsidies and Countervailing Measures*.

The third case describes an ongoing bilateral dispute involving trade in services, specifically those provided by television stations along the Canadian-

---

[3]Continued . . . .
  Institute (see John E. Carroll, *Environmental Diplomacy: An Examination and a Prospective of Canadian-U.S. Transboundary Environmental Relations* [Ann Arbor: University of Michigan Press, 1983]).

U.S. border. Although border broadcasting became an issue as early as 1976, tensions between the two countries escalated in the 1980–83 period, when the United States challenged Canada's decision to promote cultural objectives by eliminating tax deductions for the costs of advertising aimed at Canadian audiences and broadcast on U.S. television stations.

This case reflects the interaction of four of the underlying factors that affect the bilateral relationship: international developments, which in this case meant technological change and the growing trade in services; the geographic proximity of the partners; the nationalistic cultural policy that was evolving in Canada; and the existence of a strong private-sector lobby in the United States. The case demonstrates the contrast between disputes involving merchandise trade, which is subject to GATT rules, and disputes over trade in services, for which no multilateral framework exists to resolve bilateral conflicts arising from a domestic decision by one of the partners. It also illustrates a readiness on the part of the U.S. Congress to attempt to link unrelated issues in the bilateral relationship.

Based on these case studies, four broad lessons emerge that can be applied to the management of future tensions in the Canadian-U.S. relationship. The first lesson is that, in such an interdependent relationship, unilateral action by either government can produce results that are less than satisfactory for both countries. Failure in the policymaking process to take adequately into account the impact of proposed policies on the other country has been a recurrent source of tension. Clear identification of the objectives and an assessment of the external impact of proposed policy would enable each country to select policy instruments that would achieve its fundamental objectives without inflicting undue costs on the other, and without needlessly contributing to tensions. Trying to foresee and forestall is less costly than trying to repair damage after the fact.

The second lesson is that greater sensitivity by each side to the intentions, priorities, and concerns of the other can reduce tensions when they arise. Some irreconcilable differences of interest and principle are still bound to occur. Nonetheless, if conflict can be confined to the subject of dispute, tensions can more readily be confined or reduced.

The third lesson is that fuller and more flexible consultation between Canada and the United States is both possible and desirable. In the right climate of sensitivity, consultation can both provide greater understanding of the objectives and expected consequences of proposed policies and contribute to the containment of issues. The process of consultation inevitably will be constrained by such important and uncontrollable factors as the personalities of leaders and officials, and by features of the political system in each country that genuinely cause problems for the other, such as the growing role of the U.S. Congress in Canadian-U.S. relations or the nature of federal-provincial relations in Canada. There are difficulties associated with the notion of a commitment to prior consultation on all issues, but prior notification of anticipated external effects of policy can be very helpful.

The fourth lesson is that multilateral agreements such as the GATT can aid the resolution of bilateral issues by providing neutral ground and defusing potential confrontation. But since some issues — particularly those relating to investment — are subject to much looser commitments than those pertaining to trade in goods, while others — such as those concerning trade in services — are not covered by multilateral or bilateral agreements, problems can still be expected to arise.

Successful management of future tensions can be assisted by the reliance on multilateral agreements to shape the resolution of bilateral disputes and by a new framework of understanding between the two countries. This framework could embody norms and principles within which the two countries could act to limit the impact of policy on each other in instances where no multilateral framework or national legislation applies. Both countries have a stake in such new arrangements because not only is the potential for differences likely to increase in future but, with growing bilateral interdependence, the costs of failure are rising as well.

2

Underlying Factors Affecting the Canadian-U.S. Relationship

Tension in the Canadian-U.S. relationship frequently focuses on particular disputes. Although each case may appear to be discrete, certain factors tend to shape many of them. The purpose of this chapter is to identify some of the factors underlying Canadian-U.S. difficulties during the 1980–83 period and that will continue to be significant influences in the future. These underlying sources of tension include pressures from the international environment, differing political philosophies, the increasing organization and political influence of private and regional interests in both countries, changes in each country's domestic political system, and differences in governmental policies and procedures.

The International Environment

The first of these underlying factors is pressures that originate in the international environment. In the 1980–83 period, the economies of both Canada and the United States experienced severe strains due to the international recession and changes in world oil market conditions. In addition, the two countries faced competitive challenges from both developing and developed countries. In some important instances, the response was to protect domestic industries from international competition. Meanwhile, multilateral agreements on trade and payments and the industrial policies of other countries have also influenced the policy choices of Canada and United States.

As the 1980s began, the two countries, like most of the world, felt they were on an economic seesaw. The oil price shock of late 1979 came at a time when inflation was already high and rising in both countries. Expectations that inflation would continue to escalate led monetary authorities to adopt restrictive policies. The result was volatile interest rates that soared to historic peaks in 1981, halting economic growth by the end of that year. As the two economies sagged into recession again the following year, the combination of weak demand and a strong U.S. dollar increased import competition. Meanwhile, an oil glut developed and world oil prices began to fall. Tight monetary policy proved ultimately effective in controlling inflation, but at the cost of limited, erratic growth in output and of unemployment that soared to postwar highs. In 1983, a vigorous recovery was underway in both Canada and the United States. But in Canada, unemployment did not fall as quickly as in the United States.

The economic turbulence of the 1980–83 period certainly created strains in Canadian-U.S. relations. High unemployment and increased import competition raised protectionist pressures. Moreover, the economic difficulties of the period aggravated the problem that both countries faced in responding to longer-term challenges of growing worldwide economic interdependence. Since the Second World War, international trade has grown significantly as a proportion of GNP in both Canada and the United States. Consequently, international competition has become a more important force in shaping domestic economies, causing unemployment in some industries and resulting in costly, painful economic and political adjustments.

Increasing competition has resulted from several important developments in the international environment, all of which add to protectionist pressures:

• A growing number of developing countries are competing with the clothing, footwear, and consumer electronics industries that have traditionally employed large numbers of workers in both Canada and the United States. Trade barriers to restrict imports in these labor-intensive, light manufacturing industries have failed to stop the developing countries from capturing a growing share of markets in the developed world.
• The world recession has affected trade patterns in resource products. High interest rates have restrained demand, but some indebted producers, faced with paying these high debt costs, have sought to maintain or even increase their export volumes despite falling prices.
• Countries such as Brazil, South Korea, Mexico, and Taiwan have developed substantial capacity in heavy industries and are expanding their output of steel, ships, and automotive products. By achieving economies of scale, manufacturers in these countries have overcome high transportation costs and are competing with producers in developed-country markets.
• Competition among developed countries in new products and technologies has increased. As a result, the United States is no longer the unchallenged leader in these high-technology fields.
• In Canada and the United States, technological change and automation have reduced employment opportunities in traditional industries. Many of those unemployed during the recession are unlikely to be rehired during the recovery. Expansion of "high-tech" industries, such as those producing optical fibers or microchips, is unlikely to provide jobs immediately to the unemployed copper miner or copper switch producer displaced by innovations.

Reaction in Canada and the United States

Both Canada and the United States are facing — and attempting to meet — the challenges of international competition, but in slightly different ways.

The United States is seeking export growth in areas of relative economic strength: agricultural and high-technology products, and services, such as insurance and engineering. But some high-technology industries are subject to nontariff trade barriers, and many of the other developed countries use subsidies and tax incentives to promote their own industrial innovation and self-sufficiency in agricultural products. Trade in services seems a promising area for increased U.S. export earnings, but it is particularly vulnerable to requirements that firms operating in a particular country use domestic suppliers of services such as insurance and advertising.

Canada's exports include a substantial proportion of raw and processed resources; it now seeks both to upgrade these exports and to expand into technologically dynamic industries. Yet its own relatively small and geographically dispersed market inhibits the development of cost-competitive and innovative secondary manufacturing activities. Because it requires world-scale markets to diversify, Canada is particularly wary of the barriers the tariff structures of the United States, the European Economic Community, and Japan create for processed products. Another, not unrelated, problem for Canada is that of foreign investment. Approximately 45 percent of its manufacturing is foreign-owned, mostly by U.S. interests. Canada's attitude toward foreign investors — especially those from the United States — has been ambivalent. It has generally encouraged foreign investment but has exhibited concern about the performance of foreign-owned firms in Canada. The Canadian government has closed some key sectors to foreign ownership and in 1973 introduced the *Foreign Investment Review Act.*[1] Moreover, the Canadian and U.S. governments have divergent views on the appropriate regulation and treatment of foreign investment.

Multilateral Trade Agreements

The provisions of the multilateral trade agreements under the General Agreement on Tariffs and Trade (GATT) and the domestic policies of other countries will influence greatly whether Canada and the United States achieve their respective trade objectives for the 1980s. The implementation of the Tokyo Round agreements to control some nontariff trade restrictions and to reduce tariffs will offer export opportunities for some Canadian and U.S. industries but will increase import competition for others. Governments in many developed countries have a tendency to intervene with subsidies and other policies to help selected firms or industries. (The United States has sought to broaden the application of countervailing duties to offset foreign subsidies.)

Gaps in the multilateral rules for trade and investment can create problems in Canadian-U.S. relations. The current provisions of the GATT and the sub-

---

[1] A.E. Safarian, *Governments and Multinationals: Policies in the Developed Countries*, BN no. 33 (Washington, D.C.: British-North American Committee, 1983), p. 15.

sidies code negotiated in the Tokyo Round are only partially effective in con-
trolling subsidy policies (including export subsidies). The GATT has not been
very effective in liberalizing agricultural trade, in large part because the
United States sought, and obtained, the exclusion of agricultural trade from
GATT trade rules in the 1950s. The GATT has never applied to services. Both
Canada and the United States participate in the multilateral commitments
under the Organisation for Economic Co-operation and Development
(OECD) on policies that affect foreign investment, but these commitments
are weak and ambiguous. Different interpretation of their respective com-
mitments on investment policies was a central issue in the bilateral dispute
about Canada's National Energy Program (NEP) that is discussed in
Chapter 3.

Some Examples of Protectionism

The economic turbulence of the early 1980s aggravated nascent protectionism in industries that were having difficulties adjusting to increasing
international competition. Two examples suggest some of the ways in which
industry pressure for protectionist measures can disturb Canadian-U.S.
relations.

A prominent instance occurred in the automobile industry when the effects
of the 1979 oil price shock caused droves of consumers to turn to small
imported cars, particularly those from Japan. Canada and the United States
were called to the aid of their beleaguered domestic industries, already hit by
high interest rates, recession, and high oil prices. Yet despite the existence of
the Canada-United States Automotive Products Agreement (auto pact), they
did not treat the problem as one confronting the entire North American
automobile industry.[2] Starting in 1981, each country negotiated its own
"voluntary" export-restraint agreement with Japan. And more permanent
measures were proposed independently in each country. The U.S. House of
Representatives passed an automobile domestic-content bill in 1983, with no
allowance for the auto pact. In the same year, a Canadian industry-labor task
force recommended domestic-content requirements for the Canadian
automobile industry.[3] Although neither government acted to implement such
requirements, any unilateral action by either country inevitably would have
affected the other, and the possible bilateral consequences were not explicitly
debated by either.

---

[2] The auto pact, signed in 1965, provided for elimination of tariffs on shipments of auto parts
and automobiles between Canada and the United States if manufacturers met a minimum
domestic content requirement. This agreement facilitated the rationalization of production
by U.S. auto producers and their subsidiaries in Canada.

[3] Canada, Federal Task Force on the Canadian Motor Vehicle and Automotive Parts Industries,
*An Automotive Strategy for Canada: Report to Hon. Edward C. Lumley, Minister of
Industry, Trade and Commerce and Regional Economic Expansion* (Ottawa: Supply and
Services Canada, May 1983).

Protectionism has not been confined to the automobile industry. Perhaps the most troublesome measure was the United States' imposition, in 1983, of quotas and tariffs on specialty steels after a finding of "serious injury from import competition" by the U.S. International Trade Commission.[4] Canada was adversely affected even though it is a net importer of specialty steel from the United States. When bilateral negotiations on the U.S. actions broke down, Canada applied similar duties on imports from the United States.

Economic recovery may lessen the immediate pressure for protectionism, but both countries will doubtless continue to attempt to stimulate industrial development or to protect domestic producers and, in doing so, create problems for the bilateral relationship.

Differing Political Philosophies

The second underlying factor in disputes between Canada and the United States is that the two countries have differing political philosophies. Although political values and attitudes on a broad range of domestic and international issues are basically similar in the two, there are some fundamental differences, which inevitably have an impact on the bilateral relationship.

The most important difference, and one that is not always fully appreciated, is the approach each country takes to the role of the state in the economy.[5] Both have mixed economic systems, but the balance between the role of government and that of the private sector differs. Americans generally distrust government activism, seeing it as acceptable only when it creates an opportunity for wider participation in the market economy or an environment supportive of private enterprise. In fact, until this decade, the role of government in the U.S. economy has steadily expanded throughout the twentieth century, but "each new program, however important, was seen as somehow unique or temporary, an extraordinary departure from government's strictly limited economic role."[6] In keeping with a characteristic legalistic approach, the tendency in the United States has been to resort to regulation rather than direct government intervention. And in recent years, the U.S. government has begun some deregulation in a series of generally popular moves.

The U.S. belief in individual freedom and achievement, private enterprise, and the market system is so strong and enduring that it has often been projected abroad in the conviction that these philosophical standards are equally desirable and equally desired in other countries. This desire to determine unilaterally the standards to be applied elsewhere is manifested in the U.S.

---

[4] Section 201 of the *Trade Act of 1974* provides for the imposition of temporary import relief through quotas or tariffs in the event of "serious injury" from import competition. The President has the alternative option of recommending adjustment-assistance measures.

[5] See Carl E. Beigie and James K. Stewart, "New Pressures, Old Constraints: Canada-United States Relations in the 1980s," *Behind the Headlines* 40, no. 6 (1983), pp. 7–13.

[6] Robert B. Reich, *The Next American Frontier* (New York: Times Books, 1983), p. 8.

government's attempts to exercise authority over its citizens and companies globally. Its claims to extraterritorial jurisdiction have been repeated sources of conflict with Canada and other countries.

Canadians themselves have historically accepted and even expected a broader scope for government activity. Indeed, government has played a vital role in Canada's economic development. Canada's 25 million people inhabit the second-largest country on earth. The infrastructure of nationhood — the transportation and communication systems that bind the country together — were provided by government because private entrepreneurs could not cover the enormous capital costs necessitated by vast distances and a rigorous climate. The public sector remains a significant player in Canada's economic life, moderating the free market in a pragmatic way. Canadians also count on government to meet social and economic objectives that cannot be realized by the market system, including the redistribution of economic benefits among individuals and regions. In brief, the Canadian focus has been not on reducing the role of government, but on making government more effective in performing its role.

Recently, government in Canada has also tried to counter the scale of foreign ownership by establishing greater domestic ownership and control in various sectors of the economy. Americans have sometimes interpreted these activities as a form of ideological economic nationalism or as an unprincipled attempt to deprive foreign investors of rightful returns on their risk-taking. But many Canadians regard this type of government intervention as a practical way of rectifying an imbalance that, if left unchecked, would deny Canadians adequate control of their economy.[7]

In the 1980–83 period, these historic attitudinal differences between Canada and the United States were compounded by the divergent philosophical orientations of Ronald Reagan and Pierre Elliott Trudeau. President Reagan came to office in 1980 convinced that the economic difficulties of the 1970s could be corrected by deregulation, thus allowing a return to a freer operation of the market system and an expansion of private-sector activity. Allied to these goals was his desire to restore the United States to a position of world economic and political leadership.

Prime Minister Trudeau, on the other hand, had long believed that government intervention is necessary to set the framework within which the market operates to correct perceived inadequacies, and to provide for social needs the market neglects.[8] He and his government returned to office in 1980 on an election platform of increased government intervention in foreign investment, energy, and industrial strategy.

All too often, Canadians and Americans have assumed that their country's ethos is completely shared by the other partner in the bilateral relationship.

[7] See John W. Holmes, *Life with Uncle: The Canadian-American Relationship* (Toronto: University of Toronto Press, 1981), p. 61.
[8] Beigie and Stewart, pp. 11–13.

But although the two peoples have many similarities, they also have real philosophical differences that result in different policy responses to similar problems. One government's misunderstanding of the assumptions underlying the policy actions of the other can lead to misinterpretation of the policy intent and an exaggeration of the differences, with feelings of betrayal.

The Influence of Special-Interest Groups, Regions, and the Media

The increasing organization and political influence of private- and regional-interest groups in both Canada and the United States is changing the nature of the pressures to which policymakers are subject, as are shifts in the relative importance of various regions and the nature and omnipresence of television.

Special-Interest Groups

The existence of special-interest groups is not new. The pluralistic articulation of interests is part of the democratic process and has always been a prominent characteristic of the political systems of both countries. What is new is the increase in the number, activity, and influence of these groups. Often devoted to a single issue, they are now professionally organized and able to mobilize impressive numbers of votes and dollars in many constituencies, especially in areas or among ethnic groups that have previously had a low voter turnout.

Although the strengthening voice of private interests is heard in both Canada and the United States, its effect upon elected politicians has been greater in the United States. There, amendments to the *Federal Election Campaign Act* in 1974 and 1976, while limiting the funds a candidate may receive from an individual or group, encouraged the establishment of political action committees (PACs), independent of party or candidates' organizations, that may channel political contributions. Political parties have traditionally raised most of their funds through relatively large contributions from relatively few contributors; the new laws place a premium on very large numbers of small contributions, thereby encouraging fundraising by non-party groups dedicated to ideological or particular interests.[9]

---

[9] The amendments limit contributions to a congressional or senatorial candidate in each primary or general election to a maximum of $1,000 from individuals and $5,000 from organizations. General spending to oppose a candidate is not limited, nor are independent political expenditures — defined as expenditures made without the cooperation or consultation of the candidate, or his representative. The existence of a limit on support of but none on opposition to a candidate means that attack is the main activity of independent PACs. This technique can put the opponent candidate on the defensive and set the issues of the campaign. For example, it was used successfully by the National Conservative Political Action Committee in 1980 to defeat four of the five liberal Democratic senators it opposed.

The law also limits expenditures in presidential campaigns and effectively imposes a lower ceiling on them by limiting contributions to $250. This stipulation has the effect of encouraging interest groups to concentrate their financial efforts on congressional races, rather than on the presidential contest.

The amount of money the PACs have dispersed, particularly in congressional campaigns, has increased more than sevenfold over the past ten years.[10] Moreover, their proliferation suggests that candidates increasingly face an array of single-issue groups; failure to satisfy them risks direct financial and electoral opposition. The inevitable result has been that politicians are becoming more responsive to the demands of local constituency groups and more attentive to private interests, whether or not expressed through a PAC.

In Canada, amendments to the *Canada Elections Act* in 1983 took a direction opposite to that of the U.S. legislation. Private interests were expressly forbidden to make independent expenditures supporting or opposing a candidate during a federal election campaign, and a spending ceiling was applied to all authorized and unauthorized campaign expenditure.[11] Nevertheless, ethnic, economic, and other single-issue groups have made increasingly effective efforts to dominate the local party meetings that select candidates and leadership-convention delegates. In this way, relatively small numbers of people can have an impact on the legislative process far out of proportion to their size.

Thus, in both Canada and the United States, the demands of domestic interest groups may now dictate what issues are thrust onto the bilateral agenda and what solutions are advocated or adopted. Their demands are usually protectionist. Economic recovery is unlikely to eliminate them. There will always be some regions with fewer advantages, some industries less competitive, and some interests still unsatisfied. As these pressures are more clearly articulated, governments will be more likely to respond to them.

Shifts in Regional Balance

Within both Canada and the United States, shifts in the economic and political importance of various regions have added to the nature and effect of regional demands. In Canada, during the 1970s and early 1980s, the increasing population and economic vitality of the western provinces, especially Alberta and British Columbia, led to demands for greater provincial autonomy in controlling economic development. Although the focus of economic activity seems for the moment to have shifted back to Central

---

[10] Expenditures grew from $12.5 million in 1974 to $22.6 million in 1976, $35.2 million in 1978, $55.3 million in 1980, and an estimated $80 million in 1982 (Barbara R. Bergmann, "Lobbying: Shakedown on Capitol Hill," *New York Times*, April 4, 1982, p. F3.) The greatest concentration of money and power was not in PACs based in business or labor — the traditional major contributors to election campaigns — but in the independents. In the 1980 election, "four of the top five spenders among political action committees, and eight of the top 20, were groups created to appeal to ideological or single-issue constituencies" (Adam Clymer, "Conservative Political Committee Evokes Both Fear and Adoration," *New York Times*, May 31, 1981, p. 1).

[11] These provisions were successfully challenged under Canada's new *Charter of Rights and Freedoms* in June 1984.

Canada, there are conflicting pressures on the federal government both to be more responsive to western needs and to preserve the previously dominant position of the central Canadian core.

In the United States, the center of influence is shifting from the Northeast triangle (Washington-Boston-Chicago), whose politicians are generally aware of Canadian-U.S. issues, to the "sunbelt" of the South and Southwest, whose politicians typically have less familiarity with Canada. The growing influence of private interests from these areas can pose a direct threat to existing patterns of Canadian trade in lumber, minerals, and other natural resources.

The Media

Given the growing influence of nonparty groups in both countries, government leaders must now conduct bilateral relations with an awareness of public relations. Unfortunately, television, radio, and newspaper coverage of bilateral issues intrinsically invites confrontation. The transitory nature of media attention, the brief broadcast time available for coverage of any story, and the editorial presumption that what is sensational is newsworthy all contribute to an exaggerated interpretation of events and policies.

In the 1980s, the spotlight of media publicity has made quiet diplomacy much more difficult. It is inevitable that politicians' self-congratulatory messages, intended for a domestic audience, will be seen and heard in the other country. Similarly, conciliatory messages addressed to the foreign audience will also be received in the home country, where they may be criticized as a "sell-out".

In addition to transmitting the statements of public figures, however, the media in both countries often play an important role in initiating differences — or contributing to solutions. By their editorial judgment on what subjects to cover and what perspectives to adopt, the media can structure the agenda of public awareness and shape public perception of issues. The critical coverage of the NEP by the *Wall Street Journal* and other business publications, for example, had a powerful impact on public opinion in both Canada and the United States.

Differing Political Systems

Differences in the political systems of Canada and the United States and in the ways those systems have been changing recently have complicated Canadian-U.S. relations.

Canada

In Canada, under the Trudeau government, the influence of Parliament diminished and power became concentrated in a small group of ministers and officials. The way in which policy recommendations are translated into legislation also bears on the Canadian-U.S. relationship. Once a bill is introduced into Parliament, it becomes the official policy of the government. It may be amended with the government's consent, but major alterations are a tacit admission of error. Thus, the scope for bilateral consultation and compromise on policy is limited after legislation has been introduced. There is also limited opportunity for input from foreign countries or even the voting public before legislation is introduced — particularly if budget measures are concerned.[12]

Of greater signficance for the bilateral relationship, however, is the relationship between Canada's federal government and its provinces. The division of jurisdictions is quite different from the United States' and for a number of historical reasons is more strictly maintained. The United States sometimes complains that on matters of provincial jurisdiction, provincial governments cannot be bound by the federal government, so Canadian-U.S. negotiations on a particular issue may be inconclusive.[13]

The recent process of constitutional reform in Canada has prompted the provinces to seek *more* control over economic development within their own territories. Some provinces, most notably Alberta, were already using their jurisdiction over natural resources to generate provincial revenues and stimulate economic growth. While such federal-provincial disputes are the very stuff of Canadian politics, they are significant in the Canadian-U.S. relationship as well, because these national disagreements may spill over into the international arena. For example, the struggle between the federal and Alberta governments over the pace of energy production and revenue shares from higher energy prices was at the root of the NEP. In addition, a province's autonomous policy initiatives on a matter within its jurisdiction can place an issue on the bilateral agenda or complicate its resolution.

The United States

In contrast to Canada's federal-provincial friction, in the United States it is tension between the executive and legislative branches that has complicated the bilateral relationship in recent years. During the 1970s, Congress began to assert itself strongly on matters on foreign policy as a result of mounting dissatisfaction with executive secrecy and the abuse of power associated with the Vietnam War and Watergate. It imposed restrictions or changes on presidential actions and began to initiate new policies and monitor their

---

[12] Occasionally, governments invite public discussion through publication of a white paper or task force report, and recently the federal government has begun to consult more widely with special-interest groups.

[13] Nevertheless, it has been 20 years since there has been a major instance of provincial defection from a federal commitment. That occurred in the case of the Columbia River Treaty. Although the Ontario government failed to abide by a policy statement agreed to by the provinces during the 1973–79 GATT negotiations, it modified its policies in response to European and U.S. complaints.

execution.[14] Changes within the legislative branch itself have resulted in dramatic increases in staff and available expertise, increasing members' capacity to deal effectively with complex issues. The decline in party discipline has freed legislators to vote according to their consciences (or their constituencies). Democratic reforms, the proliferation of subcommittees, and procedural changes — including multiple referrals to committees — have weakened the leadership's previous stranglehold on legislation, so that power is now more widely diffused.

As individual members of Congress play a more important role, their sensitivity to domestic pressure groups will inevitably have more influence on the activities of Congress. When an issue involves both domestic and foreign policy considerations, domestic interests are likely to prevail. Important aspects of Canadian-U.S. relations have thus become increasingly dependent upon a legislative process characterized by political tradeoffs, the formation of short-term coalitions, and the linking of unrelated issues. In the economic climate of the early 1980s, the mood of Congress is also likely to be inward-looking and protectionist.

The fate of the East Coast Fisheries and Maritime Boundary treaties is an example of the pitfalls Canada has found in dealing with Congress. When Canada and the United States extended their offshore jurisdiction to 200 miles in the mid-1970s, several areas of the claimed fishing zones overlapped. In March 1979, after long and arduous negotiations and consultation with private fishing interests in both countries, agreement was reached on two linked treaties, which were to provide for joint management of fishing stocks and international arbitration of the boundary dispute. But although the U.S. constitution makes the president the chief negotiator of a treaty with a foreign government, it requires the advice and consent of a two-thirds majority of the Senate before any treaty can be ratified. The treaties were, therefore, referred to the Senate, where they were held up in the Foreign Relations Committee by opposition from two New England senators, whose constituents wanted an improvement in the terms.[15]

The committee proposed amendments and Canada was faced with the particularly galling prospect of having to reopen negotiations with the Senate

---

[14] Opinions vary as to whether these developments are merely the latest in a series of temporary or cyclical fluctuations in the degree of congressional involvment in foreign policy, or the indication of a more prominent, continuing role (see David Leyton-Brown, "The Role of Congress in the Making of Foreign Policy," *International Journal* 38 [Winter 1982/83] : 59–76). Indications are, however, that the greater role of Congress in foreign policy in general, and in the Canadian-U.S. relationship in particular, is unlikely to be reversed.

[15] It might appear that the frustration over this issue could have been avoided had the two governments concluded an executive agreement rather than the treaties, thereby obviating the need for advice and consent by the Senate. In fact, this would simply have provided for congressional involvement in a different way. Regardless of the existence of a possible executive agreement, certain provisions — especially the management of fishery stocks — could not have been brought into effect without implementing legislation passed by both houses of Congress.

after an agreement, involving give-and-take on both sides, had already been reached through diplomatic channels. Eventually, when it became clear that a version acceptable to Canada would not pass, President Reagan withdrew the treaties from the Senate. The maritime boundary dispute was submitted to international arbitration.

Some U.S. commentators have said that Canadians should understand the workings of the U.S. constitution and ensure the adequacy of Senate support for any agreement signed. Others complain that Canadians were overplaying their hand, inflating a regional issue into a national issue. Both views mistake the seriousness of Canadian concerns. The fundamental difference in the way the two governments perceived this issue was reflected in a 1980 comment by Canada's Secretary of State for External Affairs, Mark MacGuigan: "[the fisheries treaty] is for Canada our most serious bilateral issue with any country, but for the USA is simply a 'regional problem' left for determination by two or three Senators in accordance with their local concerns."[16]

This episode raised serious questions for the Canadian government about future dealings with its U.S. counterpart. Should it have to prepare itself for subsequent congressional renegotiation of sovereign commitments? Should it refuse to make any agreement with the U.S. administration without firm pledges of support from the appropriate senators?[17] The problem is far more extensive than the one treaty case discussed here, because "on matters as unimportant as Canadian relations, Congress does not act as a rational whole but as the endorser of the will of sectional clusters of senators and congressmen with a vested interest in their constituents' right to fish or pollute."[18]

In recognition of the increasing importance of Congress in the bilateral relationship, the Canadian government has begun to devote much more of its resources to congressional relations and lobbying than before. But it did not take this step without some misgivings. The Canadian ambassador remains accredited to the executive branch, and the easiest and most direct links for Canadian officials and ministers are with their counterparts in the U.S. administration. Moreover, the Canadian government does not want to generate resentment by going behind the back of the U.S. administration, any more than it would want the U.S. government to lobby provincial governments or members of Parliament to influence Canadian policy.

The Dissimilarity of Policies and Procedures

Not only political philosophies and political systems differ in Canada and the United States; often the policy responses to similar problems may be different. With two federal governments and sixty state and provincial govern-

---

[16] Mark MacGuigan, "Approaches to Foreign Policy — Differences and Similarities" (Notes for an Address by the Secretary of State for External Affairs to the Eleventh Conference of the Centre for the Study of the Presidency, Ottawa, October 18, 1980), p. 6.

[17] Holmes, pp. 65–66.

[18] Ibid., p. 64.

ments, such differences are only to be expected. They are, however, a recurrent source of friction in the bilateral relationship. Given the complex interdependence of the two countries, many actions by one government have consequences, intended or otherwise, in the other. As well, the tendency to assume that the policies in the other country do, or should, operate in the same way as one's own may lead to disagreements and misunderstandings.

The trucking dispute of 1982 is an example of a problem that arose because of differences in the regulatory systems of the two countries. Before 1980, most freight trucked between Canada and the United States was transferred at the border. Then, as a result of the deregulation of the U.S. trucking industry, a large number of Canadian companies were able to receive licenses to operate in the United States. U.S. truckers soon complained that Canadian entry controls were not as relaxed as their own. To operate in Canada, U.S. applicants first had to gain approval under Canada's *Foreign Investment Review Act* and then, like domestic truckers, prove to the provincial transport boards that their services would benefit the public. Claiming these regulations now discriminated against them, the U.S. truckers pressed Congress to enact a two-year moratorium on further licenses for Canadians. Despite Canadian protests, the new law went into effect in September 1982. Since the law required an investigation, President Reagan asked the Interstate Commerce Commission (ICC) to initiate one, calling on Canada to "ensure. . .fair and equitable. . .treatment on both sides of the border." The ICC's finding, announced in October 1982, was that there was no intentional discrimination. Washington and Ottawa exchanged letters agreeing to basic principles on the regulation of transborder trucking and promising to deal with any future problems in this area through bilateral consultation rather than unilateral action. Restrictions on Canadian truckers were withdrawn in November 1982, and the issues were resolved — at least temporarily — without acrimony, although with considerable inconvenience.

Summary

The factors discussed in this chapter underlie the three disputes that are analyzed in subsequent chapters. These factors will not disappear in the years ahead. Pressures from the international environment will continue to strain bilateral economic relations. As a result of greater economic interdependence, differences in the two countries' political philosophies and governmental systems, combined with the active expression of regional and sectoral interests on both sides of the border, will add to the complexities of managing the relationship.

3

The National Energy Program

In October 1980, the Canadian government introduced the National Energy Program (NEP), a set of policies, federal-provincial agreements, legislation, and regulations that would change many aspects of the country's oil and gas activities from exploration to pricing and taxation. Although the NEP was designed to achieve domestic policy goals of security of supply, greater Canadian participation in the petroleum industry, and changes in revenue sharing among governments, it also had a major impact in the United States and resulted in a dispute that dominated the bilateral relationship during the 1980–83 period.[1]

The issue's origins can be attributed to several underlying factors: rapid changes in world oil market conditions that created the context for both countries' actions, Canadian domestic politics that were influenced by bitter federal-provincial relations and an increase in nationalist sentiments about energy policy, and a philosophical divergence between the Canadian and U.S. governments. The resulting dispute was not about energy *per se* but about investment and, to a lesser extent, trade.

Managing the resolution of the dispute over the NEP was, at first, very difficult because of heated initial exchanges and the strong positions taken by both sides. Inflammatory public statements and threats of retaliatory action contrasted sharply with the traditional practice of quiet diplomacy and long-standing norms of conduct between the two countries. But the central concern of the United States was to prevent any departure from the established principle of "national treatment" of foreign investors embodied in a declaration by the Organisation for Economic Co-operation and Development (OECD). In pursuing this goal, it chose primarily to use multilateral institutions to influence Canada's policies.

The purpose of this chapter is to describe the origins of Canada's policy in more detail and to analyze the factors that mainly determined how the bilateral issues were managed and partially resolved. This analysis, together with that in the two succeeding chapters, provides the basis for the lessons for the future that are outlined in Chapter 6.

---

[1] The two most useful studies of this bilateral issue are Stephen Clarkson, *Canada and the Reagan Challenge* (Ottawa: Canadian Institute for Economic Policy, 1982), and Edward Wonder, "The US Government Response to the Canadian National Energy Program," *Canadian Public Policy* 8 (Supplement, October 1982): 480–493.

The NEP in Context

The NEP was developed in response to dramatic changes in world oil market conditions. These changes affected Canadians because, despite the fact that a large quantity of petroleum is produced in Western Canada, the high cost of transporting it to Eastern Canada had made foreign oil imports more economical in that part of the country. After the first sharp increase in oil prices in 1973 and 1974, the international price of oil continued to rise — although less rapidly than the rate of inflation — and many Canadians became uneasy. When world oil prices more than doubled in the 1979–80 period, however, the reaction of oil importers became more urgent. The formal description of the NEP explicitly reflected this mood:

> Clearly, the world economy faces a decade of traumatic adjustment and transformation, supply uncertainties and unpredictable world oil prices. This means low rates of economic growth and persistent inflation, as the world economy adjusts to successive price shocks.
> Clearly too, any country able to dissociate itself from the world oil market of the 1980s should do so, and quickly.[2]

Canada's policymakers anticipated unstable and rising prices over the next decade, accompanied by supply shortages in the world oil market. Their approach was to try to insulate the Canadian economy from the rising cost of oil imports, to ensure that the federal government and not the oil producers would receive any windfall gains resulting from higher world oil prices, and to assert greater federal control over Canadian energy policy.

Given the Canadian political system and division of jurisdictions, such an approach led almost inevitably to domestic conflict. Federal-provincial conflicts over energy pricing and taxation had marked the 1970s. The government of Alberta, the main producing province, wanted high domestic oil and gas prices so as to generate high revenues for itself and to bring about the long-desired economic growth of the province and region. Alberta also staunchly maintained its constitutional right to control natural-resource production within its boundaries. The federal government, on the other hand, wanted to see a much slower increase in domestic oil and gas prices so as to ease the impact of rising world prices on energy consumers and on the central Canadian manufacturing base.

The Canadian tax and royalty systems had been developed in the wake of the oil-price crisis induced by the Organization of Petroleum Exporting Countries in 1973. These systems channeled most petroleum revenues to the industry and to the governments of the producing provinces. As world and Canadian oil prices continued to rise, the substantially foreign-owned Canadian oil industry became wealthier and so did the oil-producing provinces.

---

[2] Canada, Department of Energy, Mines and Resources, *The National Energy Program* (Ottawa: Supply and Services Canada, October 1980), p. 7.

With gradual increases in domestic oil and natural gas prices, the Alberta Heritage Savings Trust Fund (a government trust into which a proportion of annual revenues is deposited for future use) had swelled by the end of the 1970s to multibillion-dollar proportions. The federal government, however, faced increasing expenditures to subsidize imports of high-priced foreign oil so that Canadian consumers would be cushioned from the impact of high world prices.

In negotiations with Alberta, the federal government sought to increase its share of energy revenues and to increase its control over such matters as the pace of development of the oil and gas industry. It also sought to reduce the high level of foreign ownership and control of the Canadian oil and gas industry.

The federal Liberal government's concern about foreign ownership was not new. In the mid-1970s, the Minister of Energy, Mines and Resources had announced the objective of moving toward higher levels of Canadian owner-ship of the oil industry, though effective measures to implement it had not been introduced.[3] The sharp price increase in 1979 renewed the fears of federal policymakers. They had a general concern that multinational oil corporations might disregard Canadian interests in exploration or production decisions or in some future world energy-supply crisis. More specifically, the federal government was concerned that because more than 70 percent of sales of Canadian oil and gas were made by foreign-owned or foreign-controlled firms, non-Canadians would reap the major financial benefits of increased prices.[4] If those profits were then repatriated, there would be a drain on the Canadian economy. If they were reinvested in new exploration, then oppor-tunities for new Canadian participation would continue to be limited.

When its negotiations with Alberta broke down in July 1980, the federal government decided to act unilaterally. The NEP, to be introduced as part of an autumn budget, would focus on increasing federal revenues and giving Ottawa control over energy policy. The fact that these Canadian domestic policy goals would have a major impact on the United States was largely ignored in the rush to prepare the program.[5] Canada's multilateral obligations under the General Agreement on Tariffs and Trade (GATT) and commitments with the OECD were also little considered.

Few people had an opportunity to point out these considerations. Because the NEP was to be introduced as part of the forthcoming budget, budget secrecy applied. Consultation with outside experts from industry, provincial

---

[3] Canada, Department of Energy, Mines and Resources, *An Energy Strategy for Canada: Policies for Self-Reliance* (Ottawa: Supply and Services Canada, 1976), p. 146.

[4] From 1975 to 1979, the Canadian oil and gas industry generated net capital outflows of $2.1 billion, including the return of capital to foreign investors and investment abroad, and paid out $1.6 billion in dividends and interest to foreigners (Canada, Department of Energy, Mines and Resources, *The National Energy Program*, pp. 17, 21–22.

[5] Clarkson, pp. 56–57.

governments, or the public at large was not possible even if it had been considered desirable. A small circle of policymakers, who clearly favored expanded federal intervention in the energy sector, designed the program within the parameters set by the Minister of Energy, Mines and Resources, Marc Lalonde.[6] The normal process of interdepartmental consultation was not followed. Entire departments, such as External Affairs, and even some key individuals in other departments such as Finance, and Industry, Trade and Commerce were frozen out of the preparatory process, apparently so that no complications might be introduced.[7]

From the evolution of policy in the late 1970s and from the 1980 throne speech, the United States was familiar with the philosophy and objectives on which the NEP was based. But U.S. leaders first heard the details of the policy when they received phone calls from angry oil-company executives asking what Washington was going to do about the program then being announced in Ottawa.

Although this situation partly reflected budget secrecy, the lack of prior consultation with or even of notification of the U.S. government had serious consequences. Canadian policymakers had been deprived of a source of information about the effects of certain features of the NEP and the likely reaction to them. Even worse was the creation of a climate of surprise and disappointment in which the increasingly emotional and bitter reaction between the two governments would develop in the months ahead.

Provisions of the NEP

The NEP had three broad goals: energy security, fairness in energy pricing and revenue sharing, and increased Canadian participation in the oil and gas industry.

The first of these goals, *energy security*, was to be attained by making Canada self-sufficient in oil by 1990. Independence from world oil markets was to be achieved through a combination of oil conservation, a shift to alternative energy sources, expanded domestic production, and the reduction or elimination of imports.

The second goal was that of *fairness in energy pricing and revenue sharing*. As the Liberals had promised during the 1980 federal election campaign, oil price increases were to be held down for consumers and manufacturers in Eastern Canada; the mechanism used to achieve this goal was to be a blended-pricing scheme that charged the wellhead price plus a consumer levy to cover the cost of imported oil that, at world prices, was originally substantially above the domestic price. The distribution of revenues was restructured so as to increase the federal government's share from 10 to 25 percent, leaving 43

[6] See G. Bruce Doern, "Energy, Mines and Resources, the Energy Ministry and the National Energy Program," in G. Bruce Doern, ed., *How Ottawa Spends Your Tax Dollars: Federal Priorities 1981* (Toronto: James Lorimer, 1981), pp. 56–61.
[7] Clarkson, pp. 297–298.

percent for the governments of the producing provinces and 33 percent for industry.

The third objective of the NEP was to *increase Canadian participation in the oil and gas industry* ("Canadianization", as it came to be called). The specific objective was to reduce the level of foreign ownership of the industry to less than 50 percent by 1990 and to establish Canadian control over a significant number of large, foreign-owned oil and gas firms. The NEP included a number of measures to attain this Canadianization. One of the most important restricted permits for oil and gas production on territory under federal jurisdiction to companies that were at least 50 percent Canadian-owned. A foreign company that made an exploitable discovery offshore or on federally owned land (the Canada Lands) in the Yukon and Northwest Territories could not obtain a license to produce from it without joining with a Canadian partner holding at least a 50 percent interest.

A second Canadianization measure was the introduction of preferential grants for Canadian firms. The old system of depletion allowances and other tax incentives for nonfrontier exploration was available to all oil and gas firms. The NEP replaced it with the Petroleum Incentives Program (PIP), which paid direct subsidies for exploration and development on a scale reflecting the degree of Canadian ownership of the company.[8]

The third method of Canadianization imposed "strict requirements for use of Canadian goods and services in exploration, development and production programs on the Canada Lands, and in major non-conventional oil projects."[9]

A more direct role for the federal government in the energy sector through state-owned enterprise was also expected to Canadianize the industry. In seeking to achieve this objective, the government was encouraged by public support for government-owned Petro-Canada as a window on the industry, a stimulus to activity, and a supporter of domestic industries that provide goods and services to the energy sector. The NEP contended that Crown corporations — and specifically Petro-Canada — should be more extensively involved in the Canadian energy industry:

> The industry owes much of its prosperity to cash flow and incentives provided by Canadian consumers and taxpayers, few of whom are in a position to share in the benefits of industry growth. For most Canadians, the only way to ensure that they do share in the wealth generated by oil, and to have a say in companies exploiting that resource, is to have more companies that are owned by all Canadians.[10]

---

[8] Details of the program have since been modified but the sliding scale remains. Essentially, all companies are entitled to basic PIP grants for 25 percent of exploration costs on the Canada Lands. The amount of the grant increases for companies that are more than 50 percent Canadian-owned; a company more than 75 percent Canadian-owned can receive 80 percent of exploration costs.

[9] Canada, Department of Energy, Mines and Resources, *The National Energy Program,* p. 103.

[10] Ibid., p. 20.

The NEP envisaged an early increase in the federal government's owner-ship of the oil and gas sector to give Ottawa more influence over the pace of development in the industry and more leverage with regard to the provinces and the industry. In addition to increasing Petro-Canada's investment activity, the program introduced a special tax to finance the government's purchase of foreign oil companies.

The most controversial Canadianization measure of the NEP was the Crown Interest provision. Under it, any company, whether Canadian- or foreign-owned, that held an oil or gas lease on the Canada Lands had to yield to the federal government (as represented by Petro-Canada or some similar Crown corporation) a 25 percent equity in that lease. This "carried interest", which could be converted to a working interest up to 30 days from the issuing of a production license, was required of all future or current leases except those for three fields already in production, whether or not exploration had begun under different regulations before the introduction of the NEP.

This measure represented the federal government's decision to increase its direct control of offshore energy development. Alternative instruments to meet implied revenue objectives, such as taxation or royalty arrangements, or direct regulation of the pace of resource development, were apparently either rejected or never considered.

Concerns of the U.S. Government

The Canadian government's attempt to restructure the entire Canadian oil and gas industry was announced just days before the 1980 presidential elections in the United States. With its diminution of the role of foreign — principally U.S. — energy companies, the NEP ran headlong into the free-market orientation of the Reagan administration. Even its relatively non-controversial elements, such as those relating to energy security, which might have aligned comfortably with the similar objectives of the Carter administra-tion, involved a degree of government regulation that was unpalatable to the U.S. government elected in November 1980.

Washington took particular exception to the way in which the Canadian government proposed to achieve its objectives. Specifically, U.S. concerns focused on four main areas of the NEP: the oil-pricing policy, the procure-ment provisions, the Crown Interest provision in oil and gas leases, and the discriminatory treatment of foreign-owned companies.

Oil-Pricing Policy

The United States charged that the maintenance of Canada's domestic oil price below world levels was, in effect, a subsidy to Canadian industry. This, undoubtedly, was partly the intention. The U.S. government raised the possibility of countervailing duties against Canadian exports and suggested that the administered price level might have adverse consequences for the NEP's goal of energy security.

These concerns were, however, largely alleviated by the federal-provincial pricing agreements of September 1981, which provided for prices to rise closer to world levels.

Procurement Provisions

The United States saw the NEP's favoring of Canadian suppliers of goods and services as a restraint on U.S. export opportunities and called it a violation of Canadian obligations under the GATT. The Canadian government intended the procurement provisions to stimulate Canadian industry by overcoming a perceived tendency of multinational corporations to deal with their traditional suppliers and giving domestic companies and labor fair access to major projects in Canada. The initial draft legislation, however, was clearly in violation of the GATT in that it implied companies would be required to make maximum use of Canadian goods, services, and labor, whether competitive or not.

The procurement section of the bill was subsequently changed to provide that, although Canadian goods and services had to be considered, they were to be assessed on a competitive basis. U.S. officials have taken some of the credit for bringing about this change. It appears, however, that some Canadian government departments that had not been consulted before the legislation was drafted were equally concerned about the original language and argued for the change during the interdepartmental consultations that followed the announcement of the NEP.

Despite the change, some aspects of the procurement procedure still caused concern by the end of 1983. An oil or gas company that accepted a bid from a foreign supplier had to explain why a Canadian supplier had not been chosen. Companies feared that this procedure might expose them to retaliation in, for example, obtaining future exploration permits. The U.S. government continues to monitor the procurement provisions closely.

The Crown Interest Provision in Oil and Gas Leases

The United States did not object to the Canadian government's reserving an interest in future exploration leases, although it suggested that this step might discourage investment and exploration in Canada. The main bone of contention was the imposition of a 25 percent interest in oil and gas already discovered but not yet in production on the Canada Lands. The United States saw the provision as changing the rules in the middle of the game, as a form of expropriation that required prompt, adequate, and effective compensation, in line with international standards.

The Canadian government was insistent that the Crown Interest provision apply to all nonproducing areas of the Canada Lands, irrespective of the nationality of company ownership or the date of the exploration license, and that the reservation of Crown rights should not involve the payment of compensation. It argued that, although the change in the rules might be detrimental to the future earnings of the companies affected, unanticipated increases in world oil prices had occurred and that it was common international practice not to allow industry to enjoy all the financial benefits of such increases. It suggested that when the United States imposes a windfall profits tax or any other tax or royalty charge, rules are also changed after an investment has been made.

The Canadian Senate Committee on Banking, Trade and Commerce saw it rather differently:

> The Committee agrees that a royalty or tax may be imposed or increased and, as such, it may have retroactive effect. The Crown's share is not, however, a royalty or tax. It is the acquisition of someone else's rights.[11]

This was also how the U.S. government perceived the situation. It argued that companies, such as Mobil Corporation, Gulf Canada Limited, and Standard Oil Company of California (through its Canadian subsidiary, Chevron Canada Ltd.), operating in the large Hibernia oil field off Newfoundland should be either exempted from the retroactive provision or given full compensation for the value of their lost holdings.

Nevertheless, the government of Canada maintained that its actions were in line with established precedent. It pointed out that, contrary to the practice in the United States, where mineral rights on public lands are sold at auction to private companies, Canadian mineral rights remain the property of the Crown and are merely leased for set periods. The Crown Interest, the government claimed, is in keeping with previous land-reversion practices on the Canada Lands.[12]

In an attempt to respond to the U.S. government and the angry oil companies, however, the Canadian government amended the legislation to provide for *ex gratia* payments, although it was quite explicit that they were not to be considered compensation for the Crown Interest. Rather, the payments would be tied to past exploration costs, payable to permit-holders who had begun drilling before December 31, 1980 and had wells qualified as significant discoveries before the end of 1982.[13]

[11] Canada, Parliament, Senate, Standing Committee on Banking, Trade and Commerce, *Proceedings*, 1st Session, 32nd Parliament, no. 75, December 16, 1981, p. 13.
[12] Since 1961, holders of exploration permits had been required to surrender one-half of the acreage under permit to the Crown prior to obtaining a production license. The government claimed that these remitted lands established the precedent of the Crown's entitlement to a share of oil and gas rights as well as its intention of receiving a share in the benefits of successful exploration.
[13] The *ex gratia* payments are calculated as 25 percent of 2.5 times specified exploration costs, with an annual inflation escalation of 15 percent up to December 1980.

During bilateral negotiations, Canada gained the impression that the payment of compensation might resolve the dispute over the Crown Interest provision of the NEP. But the *ex gratia* payments failed to satisfy either the U.S. government or the companies involved. By insisting that its payments not be called "compensation", the Canadian government had refused to acknowledge that the principle of retroactivity was involved. Moreover, the companies were dissatisfied with the amounts of the payments. They maintained that they should have reflected the market value of the discovered oil rather than mere exploration costs. In fact, the companies complained, the payments did not even cover full exploration costs because they excluded the costs of drilling dry wells.

The issue of the *ex gratia* payments proved a microcosm of the faulty communication and perception that plagued the bilateral interaction over the NEP. The Canadian government considered that the introduction of such payments represented a sincere and substantial gesture of flexibility in response to the concerns of the United States. It believed it had been assured that such a move would be well received, and it emerged from the exercise feeling betrayed because its concession was unappreciated. The U.S. government, on the other hand, considered that the *ex gratia* payments did not constitute the sort of concession that had been discussed. It was satisfied neither in principle nor in adequacy of compensation, and it felt betrayed in that the promised degree of Canadian flexibility had not been forthcoming. The retroactive nature of the Crown Interest provisions continues to be the U.S. government's outstanding complaint regarding the NEP.

Discriminatory Treatment of Foreign-Owned Firms

Of all the U.S. complaints, the one that generated the most heat was that the NEP's favoring of Canadian-owned companies, through such measures as PIP grants and the Crown Interest provision, amounted to a massive derogation from the principle of national treatment of foreign investors enunciated in the 1976 OECD *Declaration on International Investment and Multinational Enterprises*, which Canada had signed. The *Declaration* provides that member nations will:

> accord to enterprises operating in their territories and owned or controlled directly or indirectly by nationals of another Member country. . .treatment under their laws, regulations and administrative practices, consistent with international law and no less favourable than that accorded in like situations to domestic enterprises.[14]

Canada had, in fact, expressed a qualification when it ratified the *Declaration*. It had noted that "elements of differentiation in treatment between Canadian and foreign controlled enterprises" existed in Canada, so that

---

[14] *OECD Observer* 82 (July/August 1976), p. 9.

Canada would "continue to retain its rights to take measures, affecting foreign investors, which we believe are necessary given our particular circumstances."[15]

The *Declaration* provides that exceptions to the principle of national treatment must be reported and explained to the OECD. Canada did provide such an explanation for the NEP, using the same basis it had used for its 1976 qualification: that given the very high level of foreign ownership in the Canadian economy, exceptions to the principle of national treatment were to be expected in sensitive areas — such as the energy sector — that are crucial to the country's future economic growth but that have a high degree of foreign control.

Such an explanation was, however, insufficient for the U.S. government. One of its primary goals was to maintain a stable environment for international investment, and the principle of national treatment was crucial to that objective. It was particularly concerned that a major threat to that stability should appear to come from Canada, a country that it believed ought to be defending rather than subverting the principle.

Throughout 1981 the United States became increasingly concerned that the NEP was setting a precedent for the discriminatory treatment of foreign investors in other Canadian sectors and in other countries. In an effort to reverse the nationalistic features of the NEP and especially to prevent the spread of such policies to other sectors, the U.S. government worked to persuade or compel Canada to alter its position. The atmosphere become increasingly tense.

Broadening the Agenda: The NEP and FIRA

The United States initially expressed its criticism of the NEP almost entirely through diplomatic channels. The issue rapidly became more visible and more inflammatory, however, as it came to be linked in U.S. eyes with a spate of unfriendly takeover attempts of U.S. parent companies by Canadian firms in the spring and summer of 1981. Several of these cases involved the acquisition of a substantial portion of a U.S. energy company's stock, which was then returned to the parent company in exchange for the company's Canadian oil and gas holdings, as occurred in Dome Petroleum Limited's acquisition of Hudson's Bay Oil and Gas Company from Conoco Inc. In other cases, such as the attempts by Canadian Pacific Enterprises Limited to take over Hobart Corporation and by Joseph E. Seagram and Sons to take over first St. Joe Minerals Corporation and then Conoco, the goal seemed to be the acquisition of large companies in the middle tier of U.S. industry.

---

[15] Allan J. MacEachen, "Investment Issues and Guidelines for Multinational Enterprises" (Notes for a Statement by the Secretary of State for External Affairs, at the OECD Ministerial Meeting, Paris, June 21, 1976), p. 2. The Canadian government did not regard its statement as a formal reservation, but merely a qualification.

In none of these episodes could the U.S. firm involved make a counteroffer to acquire the smaller Canadian company (a standard countermeasure in U.S. takeover battles) because of the existence of the Foreign Investment Review Agency (FIRA), the Canadian federal agency that must approve all foreign takeovers of Canadian companies. The U.S. companies thus resorted to other weapons at their disposal, including legal challenges and appeals to their government. In Congress, these companies found a receptive hearing for the view that the discriminatory treatment of U.S.-owned companies under the NEP was driving down their asset values so that Canadian companies could pick them up at "fire sale" prices, while FIRA prevented U.S. firms from investing in Canada.

Increasingly, the issue became not just the provisions of the NEP, but Canadian investment policy in general. Even so, the U.S. executive branch and Congress differed somewhat in their emphasis. The administration was most concerned with the impact of the NEP and its implications for foreign investment world-wide. Congress responded primarily to the wave of takeover attempts the NEP seemed to have precipitated.[16]

FIRA and the NEP came to be referred to in a single breath for three reasons: first, because of FIRA's apparent association with the NEP; second, because of the cumulative effect of FIRA's recent regulatory practices; and third, because of the Canadian government's announced intention of broadening and expanding FIRA's powers in a fashion the United States saw as discriminatory.[17]

The United States' entanglement of objections to the NEP and objections to FIRA was not a linking of two totally unrelated issues. Rather, it was a broadening of the agenda that proved an impediment to smooth management of the bilateral relationship. The two sides often had different expectations about the specific subjects to be discussed during negotiations, and it became difficult to ensure that individuals with the appropriate expertise were brought into contact with one another.

U.S. Actions in Response to the NEP

In response to the NEP, the United States took action on three fronts. First, it used multilateral machinery to try to affect Canadian policies. Second, it threatened several kinds of retaliation. Third, it used bilateral diplomatic negotiations to seek modifications to the NEP.

---

[16] Wonder, p. 487.

[17] The intention to expand the scope of FIRA was announced in the throne speech of April 14, 1980. It may seem ironic that an agency that had been established in 1973 should not have become a bilateral issue until 1981. There had, however, been earlier U.S. complaints about the FIRA process and the legal undertakings it required of firms. One long-standing complaint was the extraterritorial reach of FIRA in subjecting to review a corporate transfer in Canada that arose from a merger in the United States.

The Multilateral Approach

In Canadian-U.S. relations historically, it is the Canadian government that has tended to rely upon membership in multilateral institutions to enhance its effectiveness in dealing with its superpower neighbor.[18] Now, in an interesting, though not unprecedented, reversal of roles, the United States resorted to multilateral forums, including two OECD committees, the International Energy Agency (IEA) and the GATT, in attempts to resolve the disagreements over both the NEP and FIRA.

Complaints about the NEP

In March 1981, at the initiative of the U.S. government, the OECD Committee on International Investment and Multinational Enterprises (CIME) met in the first formal use of consultation provisions of the 1976 *Declaration* on national treatment and its associated guidelines. At that and subsequent meetings of CIME and its Working Group on International Investment Policies, the U.S. government criticized the extent to which parts of the NEP departed from the principle of national treatment. It charged that Canada's discriminatory policies could disrupt the OECD's efforts to expand and strengthen that principle and undermine developing countries' acceptance of it. In response, the Canadian government explained the NEP to CIME members and reaffirmed its commitment to the national-treatment principle. It promised to fulfill its obligations to report and explain to the OECD any elements of the NEP that might be exceptions to this principle.[19]

In the IEA, the United States raised questions about the impact of the NEP's pricing, taxation, and production policies on Canadian energy supplies and about the ability of Canada to meet its IEA undertakings, which included maximum practicable reliance on market forces to promote production and conservation. By voicing these concerns, the United States pressured Canada to change its policies and mobilized other countries to express their concerns.

On the broader question of interference with the free flow of trade and investment, the United States persuaded the OECD's Trade Committee to begin a study of trade-related performance requirements and the OECD's Investment Committee to study both this subject and the issue of investment incentives. Discussions of investment policy and discriminatory practices exemplified by, but not limited to, Canadian policies were also raised in a variety of other multilateral forums, including the OECD and GATT ministerial meetings and the economic summits.

---

[18] John W. Holmes, *Life with Uncle: The Canadian-American Relationship* (Toronto: University of Toronto Press, 1981), p. 7.

[19] Canada did fulfil its obligations to report to the OECD. It explained elements that were exceptions to the principle at OECD committee meetings in 1981 and 1982.

Complaints about FIRA

The most dramatic multilateral move by the U.S. government was to launch a formal complaint under the GATT against the alleged trade-distorting effects of FIRA's performance requirements.[20] In January 1982, it used the GATT mechanism to request formal consultations with Canada on complaints that FIRA's export and local-content requirements for investment approval were contrary to the GATT articles regarding restrictions on imports, national treatment, and import substitution.

These consultations failed to produce a mutually acceptable resolution of the problem. The U.S. government then moved to the next step, appealing under the GATT for a binding decision by an international panel. In July 1983, the panel found that the requirement that FIRA take into account the effect a proposed investment will have on the use of Canadian parts, components, and services constituted a violation of Article III (4) of the GATT. At the same time, however, the panel rejected another U.S. complaint.[21]

The full 88-member governing council of the GATT adopted the panel's report on February 7, 1984. Prior to the final council ruling, however, Canada's Minister for International Trade, Gerald Regan, announced that his government would accept the finding and adjust the wording of the act to conform with the decision.[22]

Results

All in all, dealing with these trade and investment issues through multilateral institutions helped move the bilateral disputes to a less politically charged arena. And for the United States, the multilateral approach offered the advantage of allowing it to enlist allies in its protests. Nevertheless, use of the multilateral forums did not result in substantial changes; in general they are of greater importance in constraining behavior in advance, rather than remedying a problem after the fact.

Unilateral Retaliation

The other notable way in which Canadian-U.S. interaction over the NEP (and FIRA) issue differed from the traditional pattern of bilateral relations was in the United States' active consideration of retaliation against Canada.[23]

---

[20] There has been no U.S.-initiated case before the GATT on the possible trade-distorting effects of the NEP, but the U.S. government has announced that it is ready to prepare such a case if regulations under the NEP are implemented in a manner that violates the GATT.

[21] This second U.S. complaint concerned the FIRA requirement to export a certain amount or proportion of production.

[22] Failure to comply with the GATT finding would have resulted in the possibility of retaliation by Canada's trading partners. Moreover, the GATT ruling did not affect provisions of the act regarding the effect of a proposed investment on the economy and on employment, so FIRA could continue to pursue its underlying objectives.

[23] Various retaliatory measures that were considered and expressed are described in Clarkson, pp. 32–41, and Wonder, pp. 448–490.

Indeed, in 1981 and early 1982, when relations were most strained and tempers highest, the language of threat and retaliation defined the deteriorating tone of the relationship.

Threats by the Administration

Most of the retaliatory measures contemplated by the Reagan administration were expressed to the Canadian government through diplomatic rather than public channels, although occasional press reports appeared. These measures ranged from disruption of the auto pact or Defense Production Sharing Arrangements to action under Section 301 of the U.S. *Trade Act of 1974*, which gives the President wide discretion to retaliate against any country whose acts or policies are judged unjustifiable, unreasonable, and restrictive of U.S. commerce. The Reagan administration let it be known that an interdepartmental group had been established in Washington to examine the possibilities available to pressure the Canadian government to make significant concessions on the NEP and FIRA; similar inquiries were under way in the Department of Commerce and in the Office of the U.S. Trade Representative. The threat that apparently had the greatest impact in Ottawa was that of excluding Canada from participation in a meeting of international trade ministers scheduled for mid-January 1982 in Key Biscayne, Florida. The grounds were that Canada's failure to live up to its international commitments made it no longer worthy to be a member of the group of advanced countries engaged in such negotiations. (At the last moment, the United States reversed its position, and Canada took part in the meeting.)

Threats by Congress

The greatest pressure for retaliation, however, came not from the U.S. administration but from Congress. Alarmed by the acrimonious Canadian takeover attempts in the spring and summer of 1981 and concerned that the administration's bilateral negotiations had failed to bring about fundamental changes in the NEP, several members of Congress seized the public initiative. They sought to strengthen the leverage of the administration in its dealings with the Canadian government, to compel it to act more vigorously, to provide relief to companies affected by the NEP, and to head off the perceived threat of a wave of Canadian takeovers.

A number of bills were introduced in Congress, although it became clear after the fact that some were intended more to impress constituents than to mandate serious action. One sought to revise the *Securities Exchange Act of 1934* so as to make Canadian and other foreign purchasers of securities subject to the same margin requirements as domestic purchasers. Another would have imposed a retroactive nine-month moratorium on Canadian acquisitions of U.S. energy firms. Politicians also considered introducing a bill to give the Secretary of the Interior veto authority over any foreign takeover of a U.S. energy firm operating on federal lands.

All these measures lost much of their immediacy when the wave of takeovers ebbed. The sudden flurry of spectacular acquisition attempts in a short span of time had created the impression of a wholesale onslaught on U.S. companies. But the takeovers that had actually occurred had involved a massive outflow of funds that began to threaten the level and stability of the Canadian dollar. On July 29, 1981, the Minister of Finance, Allan MacEachen, asked the Canadian chartered banks to reduce substantially the amount of funds they would lend to finance Canadian takeovers of U.S. companies. In short order the Canadian-U.S. aspect of the takeover issues became moot.

Legislative-Executive Disagreement

The most direct retaliation contemplated by congressional critics of the NEP was to deny Canadian firms access to leases for certain minerals, including oil and gas, on U.S. federal lands. They argued that under the *Mineral Leasing Act of 1920*, Canada, by denying "similar or like" privileges to U.S. citizens or companies, could be declared a nonreciprocal country. Since the authority to take such an action rested with the Secretary of the Interior, some members of Congress tried to get him to do so.

However, the secretary, James Watt, delayed appearing before the Subcommittee on Oversight and Investigations of the House Energy and Commerce Committee, opposed the use of the act in this context when he did appear, and, on the grounds of executive privilege, refused to table relevant departmental documents. The subcommittee, in a burst of constitutional outrage reminiscent of the Watergate hearings, threatened to subpoena the documents. At issue clearly was a legislative-executive struggle over policy control that overshadowed the Canadian-U.S. issue.

Secretary Watt and the administration apparently considered the *Mineral Leasing Act of 1920* an inappropriate retaliatory tool in such a foreign policy situation. They felt that the operative phrase "similar or like" was difficult to apply in specific cases and that the litigation that would inevitably follow any finding of nonreciprocity would lessen the political impact of using the act. Watt contended that Canadian firms' investment in the developing of energy resources on U.S. federal lands brought the United States benefits. He also noted that to the extent that the NEP was driving Canadian energy firms and capital out of Canada, their flight to the United States would help to discredit the program. In such circumstances, he said, denying access to U.S. leases would be counterproductive.

In response to congressional pressure for a decision, Secretary Watt finally announced on February 3, 1982 the finding that Canada's status as a reciprocal country under the *Mineral Leasing Act of 1920* should not be changed.[24]

---

[24] The decision was based on a two-part test: whether U.S. citizens were precluded by Canada
(continued)

Results

Though repeated U.S. threats of unilateral retaliation poisoned the public and diplomatic climate from mid-1981 to early 1982, no actual retaliation occurred. Try as they might, the various branches of the U.S. government could not find any measure sufficiently punitive to compel the Canadian government to changes its policies that would not at the same time rally nationalist Canadian public opinion and impose counterproductive economic and political costs on the United States itself. In addition, the U.S. administration was concerned that it not be seen as departing from the principles and practices it was struggling to defend.

In brief, the United States could take no retaliatory action against Canada without jeopardizing its own interests. But threats alone may have been sufficient to harm the bilateral relationship. In some multilateral situations, such as a failure to resolve a GATT dispute, retaliation is explicitly envisaged and permitted within clearly defined procedures and limits, but no such procedural or other constraints exist for unilateral retaliation. That the administration as well as Congress so visibly considered and threatened retaliation may have changed, perhaps permanently, the expectations in the Canadian-U.S. relationship that contentious issues are to be resolved on their own merits. Even if the threats were intended only as a bargaining tactic, they may have created a climate in which unilateral retaliation will come to be expected and accepted in future disputes, making mutually beneficial solutions even more difficult to achieve.

Bilateral Negotiations

The use of diplomatic chanels constituted the U.S. government's third general approach to seeking modifications of the NEP. After the announcement of the program, an ongoing series of letters, meetings, and speeches registered U.S. concerns and sought modifications in both the NEP and FIRA.

In such bilateral interactions, the U.S. government consistently sought to negotiate changes in the aspects of the policies it found objectionable. For its part, the Canadian government approached such interactions with the intention of clarifying its policies and their goals, rationale, and background. Indeed, the Canadian response to U.S. criticism invariably was to try to explain more fully.

Thus, the diplomatic exchanges involved some clearly understood posturing, but also a failure of communication and mismatch of expectations. U.S.

---

[24] Continued....

from investing in Canadian corporations, and whether U.S. investors were discriminated against by exclusion from access to Canadian mineral resources. It was determined that U.S. citizens were not denied the privilege of stock ownership in corporations with interests in Canadian mineral resources. The question of whether "similar or like" conditions applied seems not to have been raised.

officials went to meetings with their Canadian counterparts hoping to negotiate some compromise in the subjects on the agenda and believing that flexibility had been promised, only to be lectured once again about the nature and purposes of the NEP. Some key individuals felt personally betrayed when their perception of promised flexibility turned out to be unfounded. Canadian officials attended meetings expecting to clarify the nature and intent of Canadian policy and perhaps to explain some recent amendment to the regulatory legislation that they saw as substantial indication of flexibility, only to be confronted with more complaints about features that they had repeatedly said were nonnegotiable. For example, Canadian policymakers were dissatisfied with the lack of appreciation accorded their willingness to compromise on the issue of the *ex gratia* payments.

The frustrations arising from these unsatisfactory interactions were compounded by the fluid nature of the agenda. U.S. complaints about FIRA were really quite separate from those about the NEP, but they tended to be lumped together as the agenda grew. By December 1981, a supposedly definitive list of U.S. complaints covered the entire range of Canadian foreign direct investment policy.[25]

One exchange of comments captures the increasing emotionalism of the period. On September 22, 1981, the U.S. Under Secretary for Economic Affairs, Myer Rashish, described the relations between Canada and the United States as "sliding dangerously toward crisis," and warned that "sentiment [was] strong in favor of countermeasures against Canadian energy and investment policies. The dangers are real."[26] This statement may have been meant to be a caution that Congress might take the matter out of executive hands and deal with it harshly if some compromise were not reached. Canadians, however, interpreted it as a threat. In response, Canada's Minister of Energy, Mines and Resources, Marc Lalonde, in a television interview on September 27, 1981, said that the Rashish statement was uncalled for and excessive and that Canada was ready to pay the price of U.S. retaliatory action in order to achieve its goal of Canadianization of the petroleum industry. By diplomatic standards, the language of the exchange was harsh indeed.

Modifications of Canadian Policy

In 1981 and early 1982 Canada did modify some portions of the NEP that have bilateral implications. On May 14, 1981, the government changed the language on procurement of Canadian goods and services to conform to GATT obligations and introduced the *ex gratia* payments in connection with the Crown Interest provisions. The original preference for Canadian-owned

---

[25] Wonder, p. 486.
[26] Myer Rashish, "North American Economic Relations," *Department of State Bulletin* 81 (November 1981): 24–28.

firms in authorizing gas exports was eliminated on February 14, 1982, and exports are now based on "equitable distribution". The "constrained shares" provisions, which would have empowered companies to drive out foreign shareholders by buying out their shares so as to increase their Canadian ownership rating, were withdrawn on April 7, 1982.

These modifications resulted in part from the various multilateral and bilateral interactions, but more importantly from internal Canadian developments, including interdepartmental consultation and pressures from the private sector and from provincial governments.[27] And 1983 saw a number of other major modifications to the NEP — most notably to the Canada-Alberta price agreement — as it became clear that the pricing assumptions on which the NEP was based failed to conform to the real world.[28] Nevertheless, the Canadian government has held firm to those aspects of the NEP to which the U.S. government objected most strongly: the retroactive nature of the Crown Interest and the discriminatory treatment of foreign-owned companies.

Canada's most significant action came in the budget speech of November 12, 1981, when the government declared that the Canadianization measures of the NEP would not be applied in other sectors. As for its previously announced intention of expanding the powers of FIRA to publicize foreign takeover bids, to seek Canadian counterbidders, and to conduct performance reviews of existing foreign-owned companies, the government said, "for the time being, no legislative action is intended on these measures."[29] Thus, it backed off on FIRA and reassured the U.S. government and other interested parties that the NEP was indeed an exception and not the first in a series of steps away from the principle of national treatment. There would be no "NEP II".

Interpretations of the reason for this move differ. One analyst described it as the outward sign of the Canadian government's inward collapse in the face of U.S. pressure and retaliatory threats.[30] An alternative view would be that as the recession worsened, the mood in Canada began to shift away from one receptive to economic nationalism.

Relaxation of Tensions

By the middle of 1982, both Canada and the United States had clearly come to a realization of the need to manage bilateral tensions better and had

---

[27] In the early days of the NEP, for example, the Alberta government not only threatened but executed retaliation against the federal government in the form of a series of reductions in authorized oil production.

[28] Edward A. Carmichael and James K. Stewart, *Lessons from the National Energy Program*, Observation no. 25 (Toronto: C.D. Howe Institute, 1983), p. 2.

[29] Government of Canada, *Economic Development for Canada in the 1980s* (Ottawa, November 1981), p. 13.

[30] Clarkson, pp. 41–42.

begun sending public signals to demonstrate the underlying good relations between the two countries. Over the summer, officials of both governments made public statements downplaying irritants and reinforcing the tone of goodwill.

Richard Smith, Minister of the U.S. Embassy in Ottawa, in an address on August 6, 1982, warned that the recent public style of diplomacy had contributed to the "defensiveness and edginess" of bilateral exchanges during the previous year or two and to the development of a wary or even adversarial approach on the part of each government. He urged a return to quiet and pragmatic cooperation.[31] Prime Minister Trudeau gave a series of interviews to prominent U.S. journalists and met with a group of U.S. businessmen, demonstrating statesmanship and moderation far removed from the image of predatory economic nationalism fostered in the inflammatory rhetoric of the previous year. By a happy coincidence, both countries changed foreign ministers, and the warm personal rapport, common pragmatic approach, and regular meetings between George Shultz and Allan MacEachen became a valuable influence moderating the tone of the whole relationship.

To ease the concerns of foreign investors and the U.S. government and to improve the investment climate in Canada during a time of recession, the Canadian government tried to ease criticism of FIRA in a variety of ways. More investments became eligible for review under streamlined procedures for "small business", and some legal aspects were clarified. In September 1982, Edward Lumley replaced Herb Gray as the minister responsible for FIRA — a move widely regarded as signaling a more pragmatic approach by the agency.

By the end of 1983, the U.S. government was embarked on a policy of patience with the NEP and FIRA. Gone, at least for the foreseeable future, were its attempts to threaten and compel changes. It was confident that the NEP was economically untenable, since falling oil prices meant the Canadian government was not collecting enough revenues to cover the expenditures projected under the program. It was prepared to wait for the inevitable revision of the program and hoped that it would have an opportunity for consultation before major changes were made.

The U.S. government did, however, continue to speak out about the retroactivity of the Crown Interest provision. Time has not made it any more accepting of that part of the program. The continuing impasse seems to involve irreconcilably opposed principles on the part of each government. Thus far, however, the disagreement is purely one of principle, since the Canadian government has not yet converted its 25 percent carried interest in Hibernia or any of the significant smaller fields, nor is it likely to do so until some company seeks to convert its existing exploration permit to a production

<hr>

[31] Richard J. Smith, "Quiet vs. Public Diplomacy in U.S./Canadian Relations" (Notes for presentation by the Minister of the U.S. Embassy, Ottawa, at the Campobello Conference, August 6, 1982).

license. Meanwhile, the U.S. government and the oil companies concerned are striving to effect a change in Canadian policy before the various exploration permits in Hibernia expire in the mid- to late 1980s.[32]

The Storm and Its Aftermath

The controversy over the NEP set the tone for bilateral relations during the 1980–83 period. The Canadian government, preoccupied with domestic problems, responded to nationalist sentiment in formulating the policy and overlooked the possibility of international repercussions. The NEP triggered a storm of protest in the United States and subsequent threats of retaliation. FIRA also became embroiled in the dispute because of a wave of contested takeover bids in the energy industry.

By the end of 1983, some of the differences between the two countries had been resolved through, for example, appealing the trade issues to the GATT. The Canadian public's mood had shifted away from economic nationalism, and a more pragmatic attitude on the part of the federal government allayed many U.S. concerns. In spite of such relaxation of tensions, however, important aspects of the NEP remained on the bilateral agenda. Little progress had been made, for example, on the key investment policy issues. The Crown Interest provision and discriminatory PIP grants continued to irritate Canadian-U.S. relations.

---

[32] [The new Canadian government of Prime Minister Brian Mulroney has recently announced its intention of altering the Crown Interest provision. See Hon. Michael H. Wilson, Minister of Finance, *Economic and Fiscal Statement* (Ottawa, November 8, 1984), p. 9. — Ed.].

4

The Softwood-Lumber Case

Softwood lumber is Canada's fourth-largest export to the United States.[1] For British Columbia, the province that accounts for 65 percent of total production, three-fifths of the market is below the border. So when the U.S. government considered imposing countervailing duties on those imports in late 1982, Canadians reacted with alarm.

The dispute's origins can be traced to several factors. First, the regulatory systems differed in the lumber industries of each country. Second, the two countries had divergent domestic reactions to the international recession, which magnified the differences in the systems. Third, private-sector interests in the United States could use the countervailing-duty process in that country's trade law. Finally, in 1981, when the issue first began to develop, the U.S. political atmosphere was already charged with hostility to Canada's National Energy Program (NEP).

The purpose of this chapter is to examine the evolution of the softwood-lumber dispute and to describe how it was handled under U.S. regulatory machinery. In contrast to the emotional reaction in the United States to the NEP, that country's choices in this case were based on facts and law, rather than on domestic and bilateral political influences. That it elected not to impose countervailing duties indicated that its regulatory system could result in decisions that did not necessarily favor the interests of U.S. producers. The case set important precedents for the treatment under U.S. trade law of the natural resource policies of other governments; it also demonstrated that Canadian exporters' subjection to the processes of that law was an inevitable consequence of the economic interdependence of the two countries.[2]

Regulatory Practices in the Canadian and U.S. Lumber Industries

Central to the entire dispute were differences in the ways in which Canada and the United States allocate timber-cutting rights on public lands. The

---

[1] In the 1978–82 period, exports of softwood lumber from Canada to the United States varied from Can.$1.9–2.8 billion per year. This includes associated products such as shakes and shingles, used in roofs and siding, and fence-making products.

[2] U.S. exports coming into Canada are generally subject to similar legal procedures. In most industries, however, the imposition of U.S. import duties has more serious implications for production and profitability of a Canadian plant than Canadian import duties do on U.S. exports, because of the differences in the economies and trade flows of the two countries.

value of standing timber for which a market exists is known as "stumpage".
Basically, stumpage depends on the total operating costs of and profits from
cutting the timber and manufacturing its products.[3] However, stumpage fees
— the cost of timber-cutting rights — are determined in different ways in the
two countries.

In the United States, standing timber on public lands is auctioned to the
highest bidder, starting from a floor price equal to an appraised value plus
estimated road costs.[4] The successful bidder receives a contract to cut the
timber for a period ranging from one to eight years, usually three-and-a-half
to five years. On signing the contract, the company must post a bond, but the
stumpage fees are not paid until the timber is cut. The timber need not be
harvested during the life of the contract, although if it is not, the company
loses its bond and must pay the difference between the original stumpage fees
and those determined in a new auction. Thus, if lumber prices are falling, producers have an incentive to leave uncut timber under older, higher-priced
leases and to work on more recent, lower-cost stands.

The Canadian system of determining stumpage fees is more responsive to
current market conditions. The provinces, which have sole constitutional
jurisdiction over natural resources — including timber — differ somewhat in
the details and administration of their systems. Here we will examine that of
British Columbia, since that province is Canada's largest producer and
exporter of softwood.

In contrast to the one-stage, often speculative process in the United States,
the process in British Columbia involves two stages and is geared to bringing
the province revenues related to current market prices. First, a producer pays
a fee for a long-term license, often for a period as long as 25 years, entitling it
to cut a specified annual quota. To maintain that quota, the firm must harvest
at least 50 percent of its allowable cut each year. Second, the producer pays a
stumpage fee set monthly by the government and based on the market price
of lumber when the trees are cut.[5]

---

[3] British Columbia, Ministry of Forests, "The Sale of Crown Timber in British Columbia and
the Determination of its Price" (Victoria, B.C., December 2, 1980), p. 4.

[4] The U.S. Forest Service calculates the appraised value by deducting from an end-product index
all estimated costs of production and a variable allowance for profit and risk. The residual is
the appraised stumpage value. See United States, International Trade Commission, *Conditions
Relating to the Importation of Softwood Lumber into the United States: Report to the Senate
Committee on Finance on Investigation No. 332-134 under Section 332 of the Tariff Act of
1930* (Washington, D.C., April 8, 1982), pp. 40–46.

[5] Specifically, stumpage fees are calculated with reference to current selling prices, production
costs, and an allowance for profit and risk-taking. Monthly, the British Columbia government
determines the selling price of the first-traded commodity (or salable product) that results from
the raw material. In fact, it considers two different selling prices, depending on the region. For
the coastal region, it uses the market price of logs that can be sold and delivered to specialized
sawmills by water; for the interior regions, it uses the market price of lumber. For each region,

(continued)

Thus, the key difference between the two stumpage systems is that the British Columbia rate adjusts each month with selling price changes; under the system prevailing in the United States, the rate is set in advance for a fixed term by competitive and possibly speculative bidding.

Also of some pertinence to the handling of the dispute were differences in the ownership of the resource, both between the two countries and among U.S. regions. In the United States as a whole, about 72 percent of commercial timberland is owned and managed privately. In the Pacific Northwest states of Washington and Oregon, however, about 70 percent of the timber is available for cutting on land that is federally or state-owned. In Canada, virtually all timberland is government-owned.

The Difficulties in the United States

In the early 1980s, the severity of the international recession and high interest rates meant that the U.S. lumber and related industries were confronted with shrinking markets. Consumption of softwood lumber dropped more than 25 percent from 1978 to 1982. Yet the Canadian share of the U.S. market continued to grow, spurred by the declining exchange rate of the Canadian dollar in relation to the U.S. dollar.[6]

Meanwhile, many U.S. companies had another problem. In the late 1970s, the rate of inflation had been high and the lumber market expanded along with the housing industry, the principal consumer of softwood. The expectation was this state of affairs would endure, with timber prices continuing to climb in the face of shortages of raw material. As a result, bid prices for timber-cutting contracts far exceeded appraised values. When, contrary to expectations, the lumber market contracted and prices fell, many small firms found they had committed themselves in advance to high stumpage costs that they could not recover. In some cases, mills faced production costs exceeding the market price of their product.

Faced with declining markets, rising costs, and failed speculation, small lumber companies in the Pacific Northwest pressed for relief. Their initial concern was alleviation of the burden imposed on them by the contracts they

---

[5]Continued . . . .

the government takes a three-month rolling average of selling prices. From that average price, it deducts an annually determined production cost based on the "average efficient operator" and a maximum percentage figure for profit and risk allowance. The residual figure is the stumpage fee. However, even a company that earns a reduced profit or loss must pay a minimum fee based on a predetermined minimum percentage of the selling price. (During the 1980–83 period, much of the British Columbia lumber industry was subject to minimum stumpage considerably above appraised values.)

[6]The shift in market shares had begun in the late 1970s as new technology increased the viability of harvesting Canada's large tracts of small trees. By 1980, the Canadian market share was 28 percent, up from 18.6 percent in 1975. During the 1982 recession, the absolute volume of Canadian softwood-lumber exports to the United States declined, but their share of the U.S. market increased slightly.

had obtained several years earlier. As industry conditions had changed, companies commonly had left the high-priced timber untouched, maintaining their business by cutting timber from more recent, lower-cost leaseholds. Now they sought to have their earlier, inflated contracts extended or voided to be spared the penalty for not cutting before the contracts expired. Federal and state forest-management agencies expressed some reluctance, and competitors in other regions or with privately owned timber reserves argued that contractual obligations should be honored. Nevertheless many contracts were extended.

Meanwhile, politicians looked for longer-term ways of relieving the firms' plight. In Oregon, Governor Victor Atiyeh established a blue-ribbon panel; its report of November 25, 1981 concentrated on the bidding practices that had escalated stumpage prices far beyond appraised values and recommended modifications of the system. Although independent forest-products manufacturers from the Pacific Northwest had raised the issue of the impact of Canadian lumber imports, the panel made no recommendations of import restrictions.[7]

In the meantime, congressional committees were also being asked to examine the effects of imports, and the charge of unfair Canadian subsidies became louder. Senator Robert Packwood of Oregon convened a subcommittee of the Senate Finance Committee for a one-day hearing on the impact on the Pacific Northwest lumber industry of both U.S. Forest Service practices and Canadian imports. As a result of that hearing, the committee, on December 2, 1981, requested the U.S. International Trade Commission (ITC) to conduct a study on the import of Canadian softwood into the United States and to compare the competitive status of the U.S. and Canadian industries. A similar request also came from the chairman of the Subcommittee on Trade of the House Ways and Means Committee. These requests may have been politically expedient responses by elected officials seeking to satisfy constituency pressure by setting fairly visible government machinery into operation without actually supporting any new legislation. One result, however, was that much of the work of gathering information about Canadian stumpage practices and market conditions was at public expense.

On April 19, 1982, the ITC produced its report, in which it explained the stumpage systems in each country. It did not address the question of whether the Canadian system of setting fees constituted a subsidy, but it did note that the primary reason for Canada's increasing market share was that its producers paid less for raw materials than their U.S. counterparts. The affected U.S. lumber firms used this report as one basis for instituting legal processes to seek countervailing duties against what they claimed were the injurious effects of Canadian subsidies.

---

[7] Oregon, Governor's Timber Strategy Panel, *Report* (Salem, Ore., November 25, 1981).

The Petition for Countervailing Duties

On October 7, 1982, a group called the United States Coalition for Fair Canadian Lumber Imports submitted a petition calling for countervailing duties on Canadian softwood lumber to the International Trade Administration (ITA) of the Department of Commerce. This coalition comprised eight trade associations and some 350 individual companies (out of approximately 2,000 softwood-products firms).

The U.S. legislation providing for the application of special or "countervailing" duties to offset a "bounty or grant" paid to foreign exporters dates from 1890, although it has since been subject to many legislative amendments as well as changes in interpretation and administration.[8] Starting in the late 1960s, Congress sought to broaden the range of subsidies that were subject to countervailing duties. By doing so it increased the chances of a "softwood-lumber case". In its present incarnation, as amended by the *Trade Agreements Act of 1979*, the law complies with the *Agreement on Subsidies and Countervailing Measures* negotiated in the Tokyo Round of the General Agreement on Tariffs and Trade (GATT). Specifically, subsidized imports from any country deemed by the United States to be a participant in the GATT subsidies agreement must be found to cause "injury" to U.S. producers before the imposition of countervailing tariffs.

The legislation provides that any interested party may file a petition requesting countervailing duties. Such a petition sets off two parallel investigations. The ITA determines whether subsidization exists, above a *de minimis*, or inconsequential, level of 0.5 percent of the value of the product; it also sets the amount of countervailing duty if one is justified. The ITC determines whether there is or may be material injury to a U.S. industry. In some cases, these investigations may be simultaneous, but if they involve a country, such as Canada, that has accepted the obligations of the GATT *Agreement on Subsidies and Countervailing Measures*, the ITC must make a determination of material injury before the ITA can assess a countervailing duty.[9]

---

[8] Stanley D. Metzger, *Lowering Nontariff Barriers: U.S. Law, Practice, and Negotiating Objectives* (Washington, D.C.: Brookings Institution, 1974), pp. 101–123. Congress sought to limit the discretion of the executive in the administration of the countervail law in the *Trade Act of 1974* and for the first time imposed countervail law on duty-free products — with an injury requirement. The administrative agency in the United States was authorized to waive countervailing duties while the Tokyo Round trade agreements were being negotiated under the GATT from 1974–79. The revised U.S. countervail legislation and regulatory process, as amended by the *Trade Act of 1974* and the *Trade Agreements Act of 1979*, came into effect in 1980, when the Tokyo Round agreements were implemented.

[9] The process involves a strict timetable. Within 20 days the ITA must determine if the petition is legally correct and if its contents are sufficient to justify an investigation. The ITC must determine within 45 days after the petition is filed whether a reasonable indication of material injury exists, and must make a final determination of material injury, usually within 205 days. Within

(continued)

The key issue for the lumber case was the definition of subsidy. The legislative history of the *Trade Agreements Act of 1979* emphasized a broader definition of subsidies than had previously been in effect.[10] The petition filed by the United States Coalition for Fair Canadian Lumber Imports alleged that the federal and provincial governments in Canada directly and indirectly subsidized that country's forest-products industry through a broad variety of programs and practices injurious to at least three U.S. domestic softwood-products industries: lumber, shakes and shingles, and fencing. The petitioners' main emphasis was on what they termed a "stumpage subsidy".[11] They supported this allegation by arguing that Canada specifically subsidized its forest-products industries through the provision of government-owned standing timber to Canadian mills for a fraction of its true market value. They contended that in Canada, where 95 percent of stumpage was government-

---

[9]Continued. . . .

85 days of receiving the petition, and if the ITC has in the meantime made a preliminary determination of material injury, the ITA must preliminarily determine whether the imports benefit from a subsidy above the *de minimis* level. (If the ITA determines that the case is extraordinarily complicated, there may be an additional 65 days.) If its preliminary determination is positive, the ITA will require a deposit of estimated duties or the posting of a bond or other security for all subsequently imported merchandise to ensure the payment of countervailing duties that may be assessed as a result of a final determination. The ITA must make its final determination within 75 days of its preliminary determination. The investigation is terminated if the preliminary or final determination of material injury by the ITC is negative or if the final determination of the existence of subsidies by the ITA is negative.

Any parties to an investigation may contest in the U.S. Court of International Trade any factual findings or legal conclusions that are the basis for final determinations or negative preliminary determinations by the ITA or ITC. They may also contest decisions to suspend an investigation or not to initiate an investigation, as well as decisions made during administrative reviews.

[10] The U.S. Federal Trade Commission (*In the Matter of Certain Softwood Products from Canada: Prehearing Brief before the International Trade Commission, Department of Commerce* [Washington, D.C., April 7, 1983], p. 17) quotes a House Ways and Means Committee report:

In deciding whether any other practice is a subsidy, the standard remains that presently used with regard to a 'bounty or grant" under section 303. However, to the extent that the enumerations under this provision might provide a basis for expanding the present standard consistent with the underlying principles implicit in these enumerations, then the standard shall be so altered.

[11] The petition also claimed some 44 other subsidies in four categories: provision of capital, loans, or loan guarantees on terms inconsistent with commercial considerations; provision of goods or services at preferential rates; grants and forgiveness of debt to cover operating losses sustained by a specific industry; and assumption of costs or expenses of manufacture, production, or distribution.

Some observers felt that these other complaints were merely atmospheric to show the interventionary nature of the Canadian state. Nevertheless, the possibility existed that even if the ITA rejected the central claim of a stumpage subsidy, the incremental subsidizing effects of other programs (such as federal-provincial employment-bridging assistance programs to provide temporary jobs and supplementary benefits for laid-off forestry workers) would raise the total level of subsidization above the 0.5 percent *de minimis* level and thus activate a countervailing duty.

owned, no buyer competition existed. Instead, they claimed, Canadian governments administratively allocated to selected Canadian mills the rights to cut timber at a price set considerably below the true market value of the stumpage:

> It makes no difference that the government provides this benefit "in kind" by selling the stumpage for less than it could receive (i.e., its true market value) instead of giving outright grants; the benefit to the mills is the same as if the stumpage were sold at market value and a cash rebate were nailed to each tree harvested and turned into softwood products![12]

Using the average stumpage price set in bidding in U.S. forest-industry regions as a benchmark, the petitioners calculated Canadian subsidies on softwood imports as averaging 64.55 percent of their value and called for a countervailing duty.[13]

A delegation from the Canadian federal government flew to Washington to ask the ITA not to accept the petition, arguing that the stumpage practices should not be considered a subsidy. The petition had been submitted in a legally correct form, however, and any decision by the ITA not to accept it would most probably have been successfully appealed to the courts. On October 27, 1982, the ITA announced routinely that it was proceeding with an investigation to determine whether or not the Canadian producers of certain softwood products were subsidized. This then set off the ITC investigation.

The Process of Investigation

The Canadian lumber industry had already organized itself into the Canadian Softwood Lumber Committee (CSLC) in order to present its case to the earlier ITC study initiated by Senator Packwood. Anticipating the petition for countervailing duties, it had engaged lawyers in Washington to represent its interests during the concurrent ITA and ITC investigations.

Thus, by November 9, 1982, the CSLC was ready with a brief to the ITC, contending that the petition failed to demonstrate any reasonable indication that the U.S. industry either had been injured or was threatened with material injury by the allegedly subsidized imports. The CSLC argued that the cause of the recent decline of the U.S. softwood industry was a combination of economic factors originating in the United States, and that the Canadian

---

[12] United States Coalition for Fair Canadian Lumber Imports, *Certain Forest Products from Canada: Softwood Lumber, Shakes and Shingles, and Fence*, Countervailing Duty Petition before the United States Department of Commerce and the International Trade Commission (Washington, D.C., 1982), p. 5.

[13] Setting the Canadian provincial governments' average stumpage price against this benchmark, the initial petition placed the value of the stumpage subsidy at U.S.$113.78 per 1,000 board feet of lumber. After adding in the financial value of other claimed subsidies, the petition alleged, Canada provided subsidies totalling at least U.S.$120.94 per 1,000 board feet of lumber to the Canadian forest-products industry. The percentage value of the subsidy was based on the 1980 average unit value of Canadian lumber exported to the United States of U.S.$187.35.

industry, far from injuring the U.S. industry, was suffering grievously for the same reasons. Further, the CSLC said, some of the problems certain U.S. producers faced were the result of speculative overbidding in the United States, not of anything that had occurred in Canada. Finally, the CSLC contended, the increase in Canada's share of the U.S. market was explained by the declining value of the Canadian dollar and U.S. economic practices, not by any subsidy.

Other briefs opposing the petition were submitted by the National Association of Home Builders of the United States (NAHB) and by the North American Wholesale Lumber Association (NAWLA). The NAHB contended that the imposition of a countervailing duty on Canadian softwood imports would cause a rise in the cost of building products and risk a chain reaction of rising housing prices, falling demand, and fewer housing starts. The NAWLA maintained that the imposition of such a duty would restrict Canadian lumber's access to the U.S. market, where it represented 30 to 40 percent of all wholesale lumber.

Despite the opposing arguments, the ITC issued, on November 22, 1982, a preliminary determination of a "reasonable indication" that Canadian softwood-lumber imports were materially injuring U.S. industries.[14] This result was not unexpected because the initial test of material injury is one that is satisfied relatively easily.

The focus now shifted to the ITA, which was seeking to determine whether or not the Canadian industry was subsidized. In December 1982 and again in February 1983, it sent voluminous questionnaires to the Canadian Embassy in Washington requesting detailed information on Canadian practices from the federal and provincial governments and from private firms. In light of the scope and complexity of the investigation, the ITA invoked a special provision that permitted it to delay its preliminary determination by 65 days.

The Canadian government submitted a diplomatic note, prepared in cooperation with the provincial governments and private industry, to the U.S. government on January 7, 1983. Besides arguing that Canadian stumpage practices did not constitute a subsidy, the note pointed out that the petition, in effect, alleged that the true market value for standing timber in Canada was the price established at contract auctions in the United States. Moreover, it said, in many cases those auction values were based on little more than speculation about the level of future demand and prices; in some instances they were also subject to noncommercial considerations such as U.S. income-tax treatment of stumpage sales. The Canadian government contended it was unreasonable to suggest that Canadian timber rights must also be auctioned

---

[14] United States, International Trade Commission, *Preliminary Determination of Injury, Certain Softwood Products from Canada* (Washington, D.C., November 22, 1982). Section 703 of the *Trade Agreements Act of 1979* altered the test for a preliminary determination to require only a "reasonable indication" of injury.

or that the difference between the Canadian price and U.S. auction prices be considered a measure of subsidization.

The Canadian government's note also expressed a fundamental concern about establishing a precedent that might open all administered prices to challenge on the grounds of government subsidization. During a meeting shortly thereafter, however, officials from the U.S. Department of Commerce told their Canadian counterparts that the ITA intended to apply the "targeting test" of U.S. law.[15] Subsidies would be defined in terms of special advantages to particular industries or plants in particular regions. Administered prices *per se* would not be viewed as subsidies.

Results of the Investigation

On March 8, 1983, the ITA issued its preliminary determination. It found that the subsidies being provided to manufacturers, producers, or exporters of softwood lumber in Canada were insignificant. "The total estimated net subsidy for each product is *de minimis*, and therefore our preliminary countervailing duty determinations are negative."[16]

The ITA decided for a variety of reasons that the stumpage programs of the Canadian federal and provincial governments did not confer a subsidy. No export subsidy was involved, it said, because these programs had neither the effect nor the intent of stimulating export rather than domestic sales. Applying the targeting test, the ITA found that stumpage programs did not confer an advantage to a specific enterprise or industry in a way that would justify countervailing duties:

> We preliminarily determine that stumpage programs are not provided only to a "specific enterprise or industry, or a group of enterprises or industries." Rather, they are available within Canada on similar terms regardless of the industry or enterprise of the recipient. The only limitations as to the types of industries that use stumpage reflect the inherent characteristics of this natural resource and the current level of techonology. As technological advances have increased the potential users of standing timber, stumpage has been made available to the new users. Any current limitations on use are not due to the activities of the Canadian governments; there is no evidence of governmental targeting regarding stumpage.
>
> Although nominal general availability of a program does not necessarily suffice to avoid its being considered a possible domestic subsidy, the Department further preliminarily determines that stumpage is widely used within Canada by more than one group of industries.[17]

---

[15] "Targeting" in this context should be understood as subsidies bestowed on "specific industries or groups of industries" and not generally available.

[16] United States, Department of Commerce, International Trade Administration, *Preliminary Negative Countervailing Duty Determination, Certain Softwood Products from Canada* (Washington, D.C., March 8, 1983), p. 1.

[17] Ibid., pp. 50–51.

The ITA determined that Canadian stumpage programs did not provide goods at preferential rates to the producers under investigation.[18] It also said that these programs did not involve the federal or provincial governments' assuming any part of the costs of production because they did not relieve the producers of any pre-existing statutory or contractual obligations. On the contrary, the governments imposed a cost for the stumpage, which they had owned for well over a century.

The ITA rejected the petition's claim of a unified North American market for standing softwood timber and hence for a comparison between Canadian and U.S. stumpage prices (even though the market for each of the end products under investigation may be unified). In the absence of a unified market price for stumpage, the ITA maintained, a reasonable basis for determining the true market value of stumpage was to calculate the residual value based on the end-product price, the basis used by the Canadian governments.

Although Canadian stumpage programs passed inspection, the ITA determined that 18 other federal and provincial government programs conferred some minor domestic subsidies since they were targeted and expressly limited to specific industries or groups of industries or regions.[19] However, the estimated net effect of these benefits was well below the threshold of 0.5 percent of the value of the product and thus were *de minimis* in terms of the U.S. countervailing-duty provisions.[20]

On March 21, 1983, the petitioners challenged the ITA's preliminary determinations in the U.S. Court of International Trade. Three weeks later, however, the judge dismissed the challenge, which contested only two of the four grounds cited by the ITA in its decision.

In its final determinations, handed down on May 23, 1983, after its staff conducted a very intensive verification process in Canada, the ITA upheld its preliminary decision. It restated its reasoning for not considering Canadian stumpage practices as providing a countervailable subsidy and produced a slightly revised list of other federal and provincial government programs that

---

[18] Within the meaning of U.S. legislation, "preferential" would mean more favorable to some than to others within Canada.

[19] The programs so designated were of three types: federal programs, such as the regional preferential Investment Tax Credit, the Program for Export Market Development, the Forest Industry Renewable Energy Program, and grants under the Regional Development Incentives Program; federal-provincial programs, such as agricultural and rural development agreements and general development agreements with various provinces; and provincial programs, such as stumpage-payment deferrals and low-interest loan assistance (United States, Department of Commerce, International Trade Administration, pp. 3–5).

[20] The ITA set them at 0.32 percent of the value of the product in the case of softwood lumber, 0.24 percent for softwood shakes and shingles, and 0.29 percent for softwood fencing.

did confer *de minimis* benefits.[21] These final determinations were not appealed, and the case was, therefore, concluded.[22]

The Case in Retrospect

The long and costly process by which the softwood-lumber case was handled was carried out in strict accordance with U.S. law and was as free from political influence as was possible.[23] Although Canadian companies may feel disadvantaged by being exposed to such a legal challenge in another country, they must realize that it is one of the realities of exporting to the

---

[21] United States, Department of Commerce, International Trade Administration, *Final Negative Countervailing Duty Determinations, Certain Softwood Products from Canada* (Washington, D.C., May 23, 1983), pp. 2- 3, 8–44. Total estimated net subsidies for the 19 programs cited were 0.349 percent for softwood lumber, 0.260 percent for softwood shakes and shingles, and 0.304 percent for softwood fencing.

[22] The underlying problems have not gone away, however. The expansion of Canada's share of the market, coupled with the increase in softwood production in the U.S. Southeast, is likely to result in continuing friction in the Pacific Northwest. After the ITA decision, the lumber companies of the Pacific Northwest continued to seek legislative relief for their unprofitable stumpage contracts. Senator Mark Hatfield of Oregon introduced a bill to exempt them from their contracts, but it is still pending and unlikely to pass, for if it did it would undermine the fairness of the bidding system. In fact, it might provide an incentive for lumber companies to secure supply contracts and then to seek relief from the consequences of overbidding for them. The companies may also be pressed for a legislative remedy to Canadian competition, most likely a tariff (although the GATT would then require compensation to Canada in the form of other tariff reductions). The unity of interest established between the Canadian softwood-lumber industry and the U.S. housing industry could be very helpful in staving off this type of protectionist legislation.

Congress may also come under increasing pressure to change the targeting criterion so that countervailing duties can be levied against imports whose producers have advantages from generally available benefits. The issue has come up in at least 22 cases the Commerce Department has considered during the past year, and although industries' argument that domestic subsidies are countervailable was rejected by the U.S. Court of International Trade in *Carlisle Tire and Rubber Co. v. United States*, a more recent decision, in *Bethlehem Steel Corp. v. United States et al.*, accepted some aspects of the argument.

Other kinds of changes are also possible. In mid-1983, the Subcommittee on Trade of the House Ways and Means Committee considered two kinds of changes in statutory remedies against injurious foreign subsidies: first, proposals to broaden restrictions, performance requirements, and permitted or encouraged anticompetitive behavior; and second, measures to broaden accessibility to countervailing-duty investigations by establishing an office to help petitioners prepare their briefs and by making the procedures less costly and complex (United States, Congress, House of Representatives, Committee on Ways and Means, Subcommittee on Trade, *Press Release,* Washington, D.C., September 27, 1983).

Such changes in U.S. trade legislation and its interpretation would pose even more serious complications for the export policies of foreign governments than does current law and might also increase the potential for harassment of exporters to the United States by private petitioners.

[23] It was also expensive for the petitioners, even though much of the investigation was done at public expense. Such costs should act as a disincentive to the frivolous or harassing use of the countervail process.

United States. The alternative is not eliminating complaints from U.S. competitors but, rather, channeling them through a political forum, such as Congress, which would necessarily be more responsive to the pressures of a domestic constituency than to the welfare or even the legal rights of foreigners.

The Absence of Political Influence

One interesting aspect of this case was the way in which the Canadians carefully avoided inflammatory political actions. They were very conscious of the possible precedent of another countervail case then being litigated involving Mexico. In this case, the U.S. Court of International Trade was being asked to overturn a negative final determination by the ITA because, *inter alia*, it was alleged the decision had been subject to undue political influence from the Mexican government through the White House. There was concern that the petitioners in the lumber case not be given grounds to protest that a negative decision had been made because of foreign-policy considerations rather than on a strict legal interpretation of the facts.

Consequently, political representations by Canadian policymakers, federal and provincial, were aimed at making Americans aware of the importance of the case for Canada and urging that it be decided on its merits. Politicians' visits to Washington were used to sensitize U.S. government officials to the importance of the issue, but the Canadians were cautioned not even to appear to apply pressure and to avoid inflammatory claims in the media, such as might be directed to a home audience. Charges by the Southern Forest Products Association — in a letter circulated to politicians and industry officials on April 12, 1983, after the ITA's preliminary determinations — that Canada had used "intense political pressure" to influence the decision, were, in fact, unfounded.

After the preliminary determination, the U.S. firms began a limited campaign to convince members of Congress to support the principle of countervailing duties in this case, but it was not successful in generating any momentum, in part because of opposition from home builders and lumber distributors. The CSLC's legal representatives monitored the situation carefully and were ready to institute a countercampaign of political lobbying if it seemed called for, but it was not.

The fact that the U.S. industry was not firmly united behind the countervail petition may have helped to minimize the process's susceptibility to political pressure. At most, 35 percent of the U.S. softwood-lumber industry, including two of the largest firms, International Paper Company and Louisiana-Pacific Corporation, supported the petition. Many U.S. companies and associations opposed it because of its potential impact on their interests. This transnational alliance of interest groups at least neutralized domestic political pressure for protectionism. It also suggests the usefulness of enlisting private-sector allies in the United States to press the Canadian case when the issues are subject to political influence.

The Federal-Provincial Realities of Canada

Federal-provincial relations surface in most cases involving Canada, but throughout this episode they caused almost no problems. Things would almost certainly have been different had the ITA decided that the amount of any subsidy was more than *de minimis*. A decision to impose even a 1 or 2 percent countervailing duty would have created dissension in Canada. The unity among provincial governments and among Canadian companies that characterized the case would have been shattered had it appeared that some provinces were responsible for subsidies that also carried nonoffending provinces above the allowable level or that some companies not in receipt of the offending subsidies were nonetheless subject to the countervailing duty.[24] An unfavorable judgment would also have set a precedent allowing the United States to find some level of subsidization in related industies, such as pulp and paper or newsprint, thus threatening to disrupt Canadian export patterns even further.

In the event, however, the coordination among Canada's federal and provincial governments and industry representatives was remarkably good. Despite some differences in the provinces' policies and levels of assistance to industry, their overall interests did not compete with each others' or with the federal government's.[25]

The Results of the Case

The most important outcome of this case was, of course, the finding that the Canadian stumpage system did not constitute a subsidy. Holding Canada accountable for not having the same system of allocating timber-cutting rights as does the United States would have established a precedent that, to export natural resources to the United States, Canada or any other country must use the U.S. system to determine value. Such a position would have occasioned international strains that are staggering to contemplate. Instead, the decision set an administrative precedent that the United States will not necessarily consider differing natural-resource policies and administrative pricing systems as countervailable subsidies. Nevertheless, the decision did

---

[24] Companies not receiving subsidies might have applied for nonoffending certification, entitling them to a zero-duty rate, but doing so would have involved significant administrative cost.

[25] In this case, it was largely provincial policies that were at issue, so the provinces' sovereignty within their own areas of jurisdiction was potentially, but not actually, a complicating factor. It is inherent in the character of the Canadian confederation that provincial governments may take policy initiatives at variance with one another's or with federal policy, and provincial governments had a more visible role in discussions with U.S. officials in this instance than is customarily the case in Canadian-U.S. relations.

not rule out the possibility that an administered price or government resource policy *could* be determined to be a subsidy. It remains to be established what types of government assistance the United States might consider to be subsidies in future cases.

The quasi-judicial process now established under U.S. trade law is consistent with the multilateral commitments under the GATT accepted by both the United States and Canada. In the softwood-lumber case, the system worked fairly and was free from political influence. Although the outcome was successful from the Canadians' perspective, the cost to them was substantial. Coping with U.S. trade legislation and import regulation may be a cost of doing business with the United States, but certain features of the system create a potential for harassment by private petitioners and impose excessive, unnecessary costs on exporters. There will surely be future countervailing-duty cases in the Canadian-U.S. relationship. The prospect of legislation to broaden access to the process and widen the definition of subsidies must remain of concern to Canada and other exporting countries.

5

Border Broadcasting

Broadcasting along the Canadian-U.S. border seems a minor economic issue, but it has assumed major political significance in the bilateral relationship. In 1976 the Canadian Parliament adopted Bill C-58 prohibiting Canadian companies from taking business-expense tax deductions for payments to U.S. television stations for advertising directed primarily at Canadian audiences.[1] This legislation brought to a head an issue that originated in the development of Canada's cable-television policy in the early 1970s as part of its approach to achieving cultural objectives.

Bilateral differences over the legislation intensified during the 1980–83 period for several reasons. First, technological developments in television broadcasting had increased the impact in Canada of U.S. cultural influences. Second, the Canadian reaction to U.S. dominance was, and remains, a nationalistic one. Third, counterreaction in the United States was substantial because of the U.S. government's desire to liberalize international trade in services and because of the strength of the private-sector lobby in the United States that wanted changes in the Canadian policies. A corresponding Canadian industry lobby was also active in Ottawa on the other side of the issue.

The purpose of this chapter is to describe the Canadian context of the 1976 border-broadcasting legislation and to analyze the management of the issue in the 1980–83 period. In itself, this case has important implications for the U.S. government's policy on international trade in services. But even more serious for Canadian-U.S. relations is its indication of a readiness on the part of the U.S. Congress to link unrelated issues, a common tactic in domestic politics but one that is considered to be inappropriate for use in international disputes.

Evolution of the Issue

Ironically, technological innovations will soon make geographical proximity to a Canadian audience of diminishing importance to broadcasters.

---

[1] Bill C-58 was also aimed at altering the dominant positions of *Time* and *Reader's Digest* in the Canadian periodical market by altering the tax treatment of advertising by Canadian firms directed at Canadian readers.

Thus, the urgency of the border-broadcasting issue in the early 1980s. Border broadcasters want to make as much money as possible before it becomes virtually impossible to make much money at all.

During the past 15 years, technological developments in the communications industry have dramatically increased the choices available to television viewers and brought a substantial increase in competition for local broadcasters.[2] Cable television has been expanding rapidly, with increasing channel capacity, first in Canada and more recently in the United States. By the late 1970s, more than 70 percent of all Canadian homes were in areas serviced by cable and more than 50 percent were subscribers.[3] Now the broadcasting industry in Canada faces the imminent prospect of competition from direct-broadcast satellites that require increasingly inexpensive dish antennas to receive their signals. Other technologies, such as videodisc, video cassette, and videotex, threaten further fragmentation of the audience.

These technological changes pose both cultural and economic challenges to Canada because of its small population and geographic proximity to the United States. At root, these challenges are not new. From the beginnings of the commercial development of the broadcast media — first radio and then television — many Canadians have gone to considerable lengths to receive U.S. broadcasts. Indeed, the attractiveness of cable television for many consumers is the access it provides to U.S. channels. But the growth of cable-television systems in Canada not only threatens to overwhelm Canadian culture with a flood of foreign programing; it also poses a serious economic threat to a number of Canadian broadcasting stations that would be economically marginal even without competition from U.S. stations.

The effort to maintain and reinforce a distinct Canadian culture, which has seemed to be a higher priority for governments than for the general population, is hampered by the vast amount of commercially attractive English-language programing from the United States. With three-quarters of all Canadians living within a hundred miles of the U.S. border and two-thirds of all programs shown on Canadian television stations being made in the United States, the dangers of cultural homogenization are perceived as great.

One might think the problem would be limited to English-speaking Canada. However, French-speaking Canadians, despite the existence of well-developed television services in their own language, are also attracted by U.S. stations. Canadian telecommunications are under the sole jurisdiction of the federal government and are regulated by the Canadian Radio-Television and Telecommunications Commission (CRTC). The Quebec provincial govern-

---

[2] For a discussion of these developments, see Canada, Department of Communications, *Toward a New National Broadcasting Policy* (Ottawa, 1983).

[3] Consultative Committee on the Implications of Telecommunications for Canadian Sovereignty, *Telecommunications and Canada* (Ottawa: Supply and Services Canada, March 1979), p. 41.

ment, while deploring this fact and disagreeing vehemently on specific policies and means, also favors "Canadianization" — more properly, "de-Americanization".

The CRTC has attempted to address the problem by imposing requirements for a minimum level of Canadian content in prime-time programing and insisting that cable-television companies carry an array of Canadian stations. But as the use of cable television spread, Canadian broadcasters, subject to the constraints of CRTC regulatory requirements, faced the prospect of erosion of their revenue base. If Canadian viewers were increasingly likely to switch on U.S. stations, free of Canadian-content requirements, advertisers would prefer to place their commercials on those stations. Thus, the Canadian stations that were to be the conveyors of Canadian cultural content would be less likely to remain financially viable.

Canadian Policy Initiatives

In response to these developments, the Canadian government developed a series of policies in the late 1960s and 1970s to encourage the production and broadcasting of Canadian programing and to divert Canadian advertising revenues to Canadian stations and away from the 22 U.S. stations within reach of a Canadian audience.

The CRTC first addressed the problem of border broadcasting directly in a policy statement on cable television, issued on July 16, 1971, in which it sought to restore "the logic of the local licence."[4] The goal of retaining cable access to U.S. stations, while discouraging Canadian advertising on them, was to be achieved through "simulcasting" and "commercial deletion". Simulcasting is used when a Canadian and a U.S. station on the same cable system are carring an identical program (but not, of course, identical advertising); the cable-television company feeds the Canadian signal to both channels so that the local station regains its share of the Canadian audience without viewers' choice of programing having been reduced or restricted. Commercial deletion means that the cable-television company can remove and replace the commercials contained in the broadcast signals of a station not licensed to serve Canada.

According to the 1971 policy statement, commercial deletion was to be phased in gradually over the next five years in selected cities upon application by the cable-television companies. In the meantime, however, the Canadian government introduced a tax measure — Bill C-58 — seen as more appropriate, less expensive, and more politically appealing. The bill came into effect on September 22, 1976. Canada's Secretary of State, who was then responsible for federal cultural policy, explained in the House of Commons the rationale behind the part of the bill that dealt with border broadcasting:

---

[4] Canadian Radio-Television Commission, *Canadian Broadcasting, "A Single System": Policy Statement on Cable Television* (Ottawa, July 16, 1971), p. 26.

The licensing policy of the Canadian Radio-Television Commission [as it was then called] is based on the ability of each local market to support with advertising revenues the Canadian stations licensed to serve it. Clearly, when revenues which would otherwise go to local Canadian stations are siphoned off to United States border stations, the CRTC's licensing policy is undermined.[5]

Section 3 of Bill C-58 amended the *Income Tax Act* to deny tax deductibility for the costs of advertising directed primarily to a Canadian market but broadcast by a foreign station.[6] The announced intent was to divert advertising revenues from U.S. stations to Canadian stations, in order to contribute to their financial viability and to support the costs of Canadian programing. Indeed, the early effect of Bill C-58 was to cause gross Canadian advertising expenditures on U.S. stations to plunge to U.S.$6.5 million in 1978 from U.S.$21.5 million in 1975.[7]

The Context of the U.S. Response

The U.S. government reacted strongly to the border-broadcasting measures because they violated two global principles it has adopted. Washington's "open-skies" philosophy envisions the potential expansion of audiences, made possible by the development of new communications technologies, as something that should be indifferent to national boundaries. In international forums, it has pressed for the adoption of international standards of noninterference with communications broadcast by radio, television, satellite, or other means from any single country. In addition, the U.S. government believes that one of the priorities for the next round of international trade negotiations should be the removal or reduction of barriers to trade in services, and it has lobbied for early action on the issue. Thus, the U.S. administration's response to Canada's border-broadcasting policies were colored by its desire to be consistent on the "open-skies" principle and to strengthen its case in the wider struggle for liberalization of trade in services.

The other major reason for the strength of U.S. opposition to the Canadian broadcasting policy is that U.S. border broadcasters constitute a powerful and effective lobby. U.S. politicians perceive that their electoral prospects can be enhanced or diminished by the kind and extent of coverage their "newsworthy" activities receive in the media, so they are particularly responsive to

---

[5] Canada, Parliament, House of Commons, *Debates*, 1st Session, 30th Parliament, May 8, 1975, p. 5596.

[6] The costs of advertising directed at a foreign market or on a Canadian station remained deductible.

[7] Arthur Donner and Fred Lazar, *An Examination of the Financial Impacts of Canada's 1976 Amendment to Section 19.1 of the Income Tax Act (Bill C-58) on U.S. and Canadian TV Broadcasters,* Report prepared for the Department of Communications (Toronto, January 1979), p. iv.

broadcasters' interests and wishes.[8] And although it is politicians from the eight border states containing affected stations who receive the brunt of the border-broadcasting lobbying, they are by no means alone. Most of these stations are affiliates of larger corporate conglomerates, with media or other business operations and political influence in several other states. The resources and persistence of this lobby, aided by the effectiveness and imagination of its legal representatives, have frustrated the hopes of the Canadian government that its policies might eventually be accepted, however grudgingly. The lobby has not only maintained but intensified the pressure on Canada to alter its policy on border broadcasting.

The Response to Commercial Deletion

In response to the CRTC policy on commercial deletion, U.S. border broadcasters took action both by making direct approaches to Canadian policymakers and by involving the U.S. government.[9] They challenged the legality of the policy in the Canadian courts, and the case eventually went to the Supreme Court of Canada. As well, they complained to the U.S. Department of State and drafted a complaint for submission to the Office of the U.S. Trade Representative under Section 301 of the *Trade Act of 1974*, which authorizes the President to "take all appropriate and feasible steps" to enforce U.S. rights under any trade agreement, and to counter foreign trade practices which are "unjustifiable or unreasonable, and which burden or restrict United States commerce."[10]

Experts on U.S. trade law have suggested that threatening to file a Section-301 complaint may lead to better results than actually filing it and pursuing the case through administrative channels, and that theory certainly seems to have proved true here.[11] Although the broadcasters' complaint on commercial deletion was never actually filed, the CRTC announced, on January 21, 1977, that in response to a request from the Canadian government, it was suspending further implementation of commercial deletion pending an examination of the feasibility of alternative means of achieving the same objective.

---

[8] This reaction may be a phenomenon of anticipation. Concrete examples of owners and managers of U.S. media enterprises manipulating news coverage to influence the fate of political figures are rare.

[9] Theodore Hagelin and Hudson Janisch, "The Border Broadcasting Dispute in Context" (Paper submitted for the Conference on Canada-United States Telecommunication Issues, Center for Inter-American Relations, New York, March 11, 1983), pp. 15–23.

[10] United States, *Trade Act of 1974*, Section 301 (a).

[11] Bart S. Fisher and Ralph G. Steinhardt, "Section 301 of the Trade Act of 1974: Protection for U.S. Exporters of Goods, Services, and Capital," *Law and Policy in International Business* 14 (1982): 578. Fisher represented the border broadcasters at this time and during the subsequent Section-301 complaint during the 1978–80 period. This section relies heavily on his description of the case, on 591–592 and 641–652.

However, the broadcasters' challenge in the Canadian courts was, in fact, unsuccessful. In 1978, several months after the decision to suspend further commercial deletion, the Supreme Court of Canada ruled that the CRTC did indeed have the legal authority to impose commercial deletion.

The Challenge to Bill C-58

In response to Bill C-58, the U.S. border broadcasters took action on a number of fronts. They returned to the tactic of filing a complaint under Section 301 of the U.S. Trade Act of 1974. They lobbied Congress to prevent Canada's being specified as an exception in new laws denying tax deductibility for conventions held outside the United States, and they sought to link the border-broadcasting issue to other Canadian-U.S. questions.

The Section-301 Complaint

Mere threats of a Section-301 complaint proved insufficient to divert Canadian policy this time, so on August 29, 1978, a group of 15 of the 22 afflicted broadcasters filed one.[12] The complaint argued that Bill C-58 was unreasonable, unjustifiable, discriminatory, and a burden to U.S. commerce.[13] U.S. border broadcasters, it claimed, provided benefits to Canada — including television programing, which Canadian viewers enjoy, and access to a wider advertising audience for Canadian businesses — that formed the basis of the Canadian cable-television industry. The broadcasters argued that raising firms' cost of advertising on U.S. stations amounted to an effective tax subsidy to Canadian stations, which would result in the U.S. broadcasters' not being adequately compensated for their programs. Furthermore, they claimed, the level of this discriminatory tax subsidy was unduly high and therefore unreasonable; by doubling the cost to a Canadian advertiser of a commercial broadcast on a U.S. station, Bill C-58 imposed the equivalent of a 100 percent duty, which is confiscatory.

The border broadcasters also argued that although the ostensible plan was that the redirected advertising revenues would be used to finance Canadian programing, this had not happened. In any event, they alleged, the amount of advertising revenues involved was insufficient to establish the viability and international competitiveness of domestic Canadian programing. The border broadcasters further argued that since they could not withdraw their services,

---

[12] The other seven stations apparently did not wish to provoke more extreme action by the Canadian government, or did not favor the retaliatory remedies called for in the complaint.

[13] The core of the complaint was that Bill C-58 was unreasonable. Additional points were based on a number of legal technicalities, including the bill's incompatability with the Organisation for Economic Co-operation and Development code on trade in "invisibles" and an analogy to the stipulation in Article IV of the General Agreement on Tariffs and Trade (GATT) that countries wishing to restrict the import of foreign films for cultural reasons must use screen quotas.

it was unreasonable that the opportunity to earn compensation from them was being systematically denied. Finally, they argued, Canadian policy was unreasonable because it was not reciprocal of the open U.S. treatment of Canadian border broadcasters.

The U.S. border broadcasters' complaint suggested four possible responses to Bill C-58. The remedy they preferred was a goods-oriented response: that the President impose specific duties or quantitative restrictions on all Canadian exports of feature films and records to the United States. The second proposed remedy, a service-oriented response, was tax legislation — mirroring that imposed by Canada — to prevent U.S. taxpayers from deducting as a business expense the cost of advertising on Canadian television and radio stations. The third proposal, another service-oriented response, was that Congress link border broadcasting with the convention-tax issue, continuing to deny Canada special relief from a new tax provision that limited the deductibility of expenses for meetings outside the United States.[14] The fourth proposal was for a general-linkage response, to "consider the unjustifiable, unreasonable, and discriminatory nature of Bill C-58 when dealing with the Canadians on other matters of mutual concern, such as the allocation of fishing rights."[15]

In suggesting these responses, the border broadcasters' goal seems not to have been getting retaliatory legislation passed but rather bringing about a change in Bill C-58 to their benefit.

In response to the complaint, Canadian broadcasters and cable-television operators argued before the Section-301 committee that U.S. television stations were not licensed by the CRTC to serve Canada and had no rights to sell advertising to Canadians. Any advertising revenues they received from Canada were windfall gains, obtained by the good fortune of their location near the Canadian border.

The Canadians also argued that Section 301 did not apply to this case, because television advertising is not a service "associated with the international trade," as specified in the *Trade Act of 1974*. Furthermore, they said, broadcasting is a regulated industry and, therefore, was not covered by Section 301. Thus, as a matter of cultural, taxation, and social policy, Bill C-58 was outside the reach of Section 301. Since the domestic laws of neither Canada nor the United States require cable-television companies to pay broadcasters for their signals, the stations had no right to compensation for the "use" of signals on cable; in fact, said the Canadians, the real complaint of the border broadcasters concerned the nature of cable television, rather

---

[14] Section 602 of the *Tax Reform Act of 1976* limited eligible deductions to a maximum of two conventions held outside the United States per year and imposed a ceiling on the amount of deductions. The intent of the legislation was to deter U.S. groups from holding conventions outside the country.

[15] Fisher and Steinhardt, 648.

than the nature of Bill C-58. Finally, the Canadians claimed that Bill C-58 was not discriminatory and that it was justified by the need for revenues to produce the domestic programing necessary to meet Canadian-content requirements.

While the complaint was still under consideration, the *Trade Act of 1974* was amended by the *Trade Agreements Act of 1979*, making it more explicit that Section 301 covers broadcasting services. As the report of the U.S. Senate Finance Committee made plain:

> the term "commerce" in Section 301 includes all services associated with international trade, not just the provision of those services with respect to international trade in merchandise. What is comprehended in the term commerce includes international trade in services, as, for example, the provision of broadcasting, banking, and insurance services across national boundaries.[16]

This amendment thus eliminated any uncertainty about whether or not Section 301 applied to this case. On July 21, 1980, after protracted consideration, the Section-301 committee delivered its finding that Bill C-58 was an unreasonable burden on U.S. commerce, because, in effect, it placed on the U.S. companies involved the costs of strengthening Canada's broadcasting industry.

Mirror Tax Legislation

At this point, the center of action shifted from the administrative procedures of the executive branch to Congress. The action the Section-301 committee recommended in response to Bill C-58 was the mildest of the four alternatives proposed by the petitioners: that the United States enact mirror tax legislation. On July 25, 1980, the U.S. Trade Representative, Reuben Askew, concurred in this decision, and recommended the committee's proposal to President Carter, who urged Congress to pass such legislation. But the legislation died when Congress recessed that December. The whole issue was then inherited by the Reagan administration, whose response was the same as its predecessor's. Bill C-58 was again determined to be unreasonable under Section 301, and again mirror tax legislation was seen as an appropriate response. On November 17, 1981, President Reagan requested that Congress deny income-tax deductions for advertising directed at U.S. markets but broadcast on Canadian stations.

For the U.S. administration, the mirror tax legislation was an end in itself, to demonstrate the seriousness and effectiveness of the Section-301 process. For the border broadcasters, however, it was only a means of threatening the Canadian government. Its passage could bring them no benefit other than some intangible satisfaction. Accordingly, they did not press for its passage

---

[16] Ibid., 589.

but sought to keep it on the table while raising the stakes through the introduction of new and costly linkages.

Linkage with the Convention-Tax Issue

The border broadcasters had earlier lobbied Congress to act on their behalf by linking Bill C-58 to the issue of tax deductions for conventions in foreign countries. The general sense in Congress, actively reinforced by the border broadcasters, was that it was inconsistent for the Canadian government to request relief from a restriction in U.S. tax law and at the same time claim that a tax policy of its own was nonnegotiable. Although the Carter administration supported a Canadian exemption from the convention-tax provisions, Congress acted in various ways to defeat proposed legislation to provide an exemption, at least until negotiations were under way on the border-broadcasting issue.

In April 1977, the Senate defeated an amendment to the *Tax Reduction and Simplification Act of 1977* that would have exempted all North America from the foreign-convention tax provisions. In October 1978, the House Ways and Means Committee considered an exemption for North America, but voted to deny it to any country that had an income-tax law with provisions such as those of Bill C-58 and was unwilling to negotiate them. On May 15, 1980, the Senate Finance Committee, examining a proposal to exempt Canada and Mexico from the foreign-convention rules, deferred action until the President had acted on the recommendations of the Section-301 committee in the border-broadcasting case.

The protracted process of negotiating and revising the Canada-U.S. Tax Treaty — which contained a provision removing restrictions on the deduction of convention expenses — was also tied to the border-broadcasting question in congressional hearings.[17] The economic costs of not obtaining the exemption were an estimated $100 million per year in lost hotel bookings. Yet the Canadian government refused to succumb to pressure to change Bill C-58. It continued, however, to press for relief on the convention-tax issue. Finally and unexpectedly, on December 15, 1980, in the flurry of legislation prior to dissolution, Congress passed a bill long supported by the Carter administration to allow U.S. citizens to deduct the costs of attending meetings in Canada and Mexico in the same way that they could for conventions in the United States.

Linkage with Other Issues in the Bilateral Relationship

Having lost the lever of the convention-tax exemption, the border broadcasters searched for some other issue to link to Bill C-58 to achieve their

---

[17] At the end of 1983 the tax treaty had still not been ratified, largely because of other issues, such as the capital-gains provision.

purposes. They thought they had found one in Telidon: Canadian-developed videotex technology. With it, Canada hopes to claim a $1.6 billion share of the estimated U.S.$12 billion videotex market by 1990.

On June 15, 1982, Senator Daniel P. Moynihan of New York announced that since Canada had indicated mirror tax legislation alone would not move it from its six-year-old position that Bill C-58 was nonnegotiable, he would introduce an amendment to strengthen the U.S. hand. The senator's amendment would have denied a tax deduction to U.S. businesses purchasing Telidon so long as Bill C-58 remained unchanged. The threat was enormously alarming to government and industry in Canada, but the amendment was, in fact, never introduced.

In fact, with the dissolution of Congress in December 1982, the proposed mirror tax legislation died once again. It appears that Senator Moynihan underestimated or was misinformed about the degree of opposition to his amendment within the U.S. business community. Communications giants such as IBM, AT&T, Time-Life, and Times Mirror Co. had already invested too much in the development of Telidon technology to be willing to see it excluded from the United States.

Their opposition may have prevented the Telidon amendment from being introduced and formally debated and certainly made it extremely unlikely that the Telidon amendment will be resurrected in another linkage exercise. The border broadcasters and their political allies will have to find some other measure with which to put pressure on Canada, but, of course, there many candidates. There has already been a delay in ratification of the tax treaty, as well as the introduction of legislation to restrict foreign ownership of cable-television operations in the United States.

The Search for a Solution

Although the border-broadcasting issue seemed to have reached an impasse by the end of the 1980–83 period, informal negotiations got under way in 1983 to explore the possibility of compromise. Since 1976, a number of compromises have been suggested, but none has been accepted. Some U.S. border broadcasters offered to establish Canadian subsidiaries through which they would channel at least half their Canadian-generated revenue, thus making it subject to Canadian income tax. The gains to Canada, however, would have been only a fraction of those accruing under Bill C-58. Another proposal was for the border broadcasters to allocate a certain percentage of their Canadian-generated advertising revenues to a fund for Canadian programing, but it was judged that this measure too would contribute less than the amount potentially available under Bill C-58.[18]

In early 1983, however, Canada announced a new National Broadcasting Strategy — in effect, an invitation to the United States to negotiate on a

---

[18] Donner and Lazar, pp. III-33 – III-36.

number of previously nonnegotiable issues, including Bill C-58.[19] As yet, no comprehensive agenda has been worked out, and no formal issue-specific negotiations have begun. Nevertheless, some informal discussions about the border-broadcasting question have taken place. The initial proposal was 50 percent tax deductibility for advertising on U.S. stations, which is less than the border advertisers enjoyed before 1976 but more than they have had since then. More recently, discussions have focused on an inherently plausible formula of tax deductions calculated separately for each station in proportion to the percentage of its viewing audience that is in the United States.

In June 1983, these discussions slowed when Canada's Department of Communications informed the U.S. negotiators that it was commissioning a follow-up study to determine Bill C-58's economic impact to date on the Canadian broadcasting industry, as well as the potential impact of the proposed compromise. The U.S. government, while agreeing to assist in the collection of data from broadcasters on its side of the border to provide a basis for future bilateral discussions, in general has reacted negatively to the study. It perceives the study as a device to break off negotiations, since the Canadian government will be less likely to proceed with finding a compromise if the study shows the effects of Bill C-58 to have been anything but negligible.

The U.S. reaction, however, may be premature. It would be irresponsible for the Canadian government to make even cosmetic changes in its policy without being fully aware of the facts of the current situation. More important, the reaction may be based on a common U.S. presumption that Canadian officials have the same latitude to negotiate as do their U.S. counterparts. (In fact, much more authority rests at the ministerial level in Canada.) Nevertheless, in August 1983, the U.S. administration reintroduced mirror tax legislation in Congress for the third time, in the vain hope that it would receive speedy passage to complete the Section-301 process.

In any event, if Canada and the United States can agree on prorated deductions — or some other compromise, such as differentiated deductions for local, spot, national, and multinational advertising on locally originated, syndicated, and network programing — a festering sore on the bilateral relationship will have been healed.[20] What is needed is a compromise that allows the Canadian government to appear to have maintained its principle but that gives the border broadcasters access to an acceptable level of Canadian advertising revenues. If such a compromise is not now possible, U.S. pressure on Canada will continue, quite possibly by linking the border-broadcasting issue to some other matter in a way that is injurious to Canada's interests. Since the economic costs of the convention-tax-exemption issue

---

[19] Other such matters include copyright, satellite broadcasting, and the nonexclusivity of programs.

[20] Hagelin and Janisch, p. 23.

were clearly insufficient to impel the Canadian government to change Bill C-58, one can only expect that issues linked to border broadcasting in the future will involve even higher stakes. The border-broadcasting lobby has demonstrated its persistence and effectiveness beyond any doubt.

Broader Repercussions

Like a pebble cast into a pond, the border-broadcasting case has created ripples that have spread surprisingly far. The case reveals fascinating differences of perceptions and interest among the various parties involved in the two countries and also suggests some consequences of using the linkage of unrelated issues in bilateral negotiations.

The Identification of Cultural and Economic Issues

The most obvious difference in perception is between the Canadian characterization of the issue as cultural and the U.S. characterization of it as economic. The contrast, however, is not quite so clear cut. The Canadian argument that Bill C-58 is purely a cultural policy ignores the fact that the government could have chosen to reach its cultural objective by other, less discriminatory means. For example, it could have used general revenues to subsidize Canadian programing without decreasing the income of the U.S. border broadcasters. Rather, within the cultural context of the bill, it chose to serve explicitly economic purposes as well by directing financial support to precarious Canadian broadcasters. The refusal to admit the partially economic character of Bill C-58 imposes a rigidity on Canadian policy that is not conducive to compromise.

On the U.S. side, reluctance or inability to recognize the genuine Canadian cultural concerns and objectives that underlie Bill C-58 and determination to treat the issue purely as a trade dispute widen the gap between the two governments and elicit intransigence rather than conciliation.

Goals of the Various Parties

The case is also interesting in what it reveals about the interests and expectations of the various parties. The Canadian government clearly underestimated the strength and perseverance of the border-broadcasting lobby in the United States. It had hoped from the outset that the border broadcasters would eventually reconcile themselves to the new legal reality and cease their opposition to Bill C-58. They have not done so. If anything, their pressure on Canada to change its policy has intensified. The approximately U.S.$20 million per year in advertising revenues at issue has generated a surprisingly long-lasting campaign of transnational activity and congressional lobbying that, in turn, has threatened much larger economic interests in Canada.

The border-broadcasting lobby has proved more durable and effective than expected for several reasons. First, there is a perception in the U.S. political system that politicians can be made or broken by the media coverage they receive. Second, the absence of any U.S. "hostages" in Canada — unlike the situation of the oil companies in the case of the National Energy Program — means that most of the border broadcasters are not concerned about the Canadian government's reaction. Third, the lobby employed imaginative legal representatives. Though the border broadcasters have not been entirely united — some did not participate in the Section-301 complaint — they have had a continuing influence in Congress. Finally, the case has offered little scope for countervailing lobbying by U.S. private-sector interests supportive of the Canadian position. On the proposed Telidon amendment, the communications giants who wish to avail themselves of that technology made their power evident, but no other issue has elicited much support for Canada's stand.

Within the United States, there is a clear difference of interest between the administration and the border broadcasters, though both are opposed to Bill C-58. The latter want to get Bill C-58 changed so as to bring them more revenue from their Canadian viewers. They see the introduction — and not especially the passage — of mirror tax legislation and attached, unrelated amendments as a club that may threaten Canadian interests into impelling their government to modify its policy.

The U.S. administration, on the other hand, sees the border-broadcasting issue as a test of using Section 301 in dealing with trade in services. It is a precedent-setting case — the only example of proposed unilateral mirror tax legislation not associated with a violation of some multilateral agreement. The administration's concern is that this legislation has been introduced three times, by two presidents. Failure to pass it would show the Section-301 process to be toothless. It would also set a precedent contrary to the firm stand on trade in services the administration wants to present to back up its efforts to generate international support for the global liberalization of trade in services under the GATT.

Accordingly, in the absence of any compromise solution, the U.S. administration is far more likely than the border broadcasters to press for early passage of mirror tax legislation. At the end of 1983, it remained an open question whether Congress would be more responsive to the executive branch or to the border-broadcasting lobby on this issue.

Successive administrations have already disappointed the border broadcasters. Although the Section-301 committee did find Bill C-58 to be an unreasonable restriction on U.S. trade in services, the broadcasters saw the committee's proposed legislative remedy of a mirror tax bill as less desirable than the imposition of direct duties or quotas on Canadian exports of films and records to the United States. Similarly, although Section 301 authorizes the President to take all appropriate and feasible action, the administration's handling of the this case suggests that it is not necessarily willing to impose restrictions on the import of goods in retaliation for restriction on trade in services.[21] The resort to a legislative response involves a loss of control over the process for both the administration and the private-sector complainants, but it does open opportunities for protracted lobbying of Congress to amend the retaliatory legislation. This pressure creates another level of the threats and posturing that are the main effect of Section 301, whose true purpose is not to retaliate, but to effect change in foreign trade restrictions.

Linkage in Bilateral Relations

This case also stands out in Canadian-U.S. relations as an instance of repeated linkages of unrelated issues. Both governments have traditionally argued that such linkage escalates confrontation, discourages cooperation, and creates an environment in which one participant can only gain at another's expense. Hence, such linkages have been avoided, by mutual agreement, in government-to-government negotiations. Yet this case also shows that the traditional reasoning may not sway those who pursue specific interests without regard for the long-term bilateral relationship. In fact, they may find linkage an appealing tactic.

Of course, linkage does not just happen. Issues are consciously linked by those involved. In the border-broadcasting case, it was lawyers working for the U.S. broadcasters who came up with the ideas of linking Bill C-58 to the convention issue, to fishing rights, to Telidon, to the tax treaty, and so on. Now the genie is out of the bottle. As other issues arise in the bilateral relationship, private-interest groups are likely to press for linkages, especially when dealing with Congress, where tradeoffs and the linkage of issues in the domestic arena are common occurrences.

---

[21] Fisher and Steinhardt, 650.

6

Managing Tensions in Bilateral Relations

The preceding chapters have illustrated the ways in which fundamental influences in the Canadian-U.S. relationship determined both the nature of a series of critical problems during the 1980–83 period and the methods by which they were handled. Pressures from the international economic environment, differences in political philosophy, and the dissimilarity of policies and procedures all played a role. Adding to the pressures were the increasing political influence of private and regional interests in both countries, as well as changes in their domestic political systems. These factors are likely to continue to be sources of instability and tension in the years ahead.

Thus, the Canadian-U.S. relationship is now in transition. If it is to move smoothly to a new phase, policymaking will have to be more sensitive, flexible, and geared to a longer time frame, taking into account the fundamental influences that shape the relationship and the anticipated impact of policy decisions. It should be possible to learn from the experiences of the early 1980s and to apply that understanding to the handling of future differences so that costly disagreements are kept to a minimum.

Lessons from the 1980–83 Period

When differences arise in the bilateral relationship, the very fact that the two countries are so closely linked makes it more likely that they will cooperate with each other to their mutual benefit. Those conflicts that are difficult to resolve may at least be limited in magnitude by the interdependence. But once either partner thinks in terms of winning or losing, the result is likely to be confrontation and behavior aimed at unilateral advantage rather than mutual benefit.

From the three cases examined in this study, one can draw a number of conclusions that are applicable to the future conduct of the relationship.

• *In an interdependent relationship, unilateral action by either government can produce results that are less than satisfactory to both.*

Each of the three cases examined in this study involved unilateral attempts to alter transborder flows of investment, trade, or communications. Because of the interdependent relationship, each of these changes inevitably affected the interests of the other country. Unilateral action may be taken, as it was in the

National Energy Program (NEP) and border-broadcasting cases, because one partner considers its own national objectives to be so important that the consequences for the relationship are secondary. Ironically, during the period, it was Canada, the smaller partner in this asymmetrical relationship, that took unilateral action to achieve domestic objectives, but with far-reaching consequences for both partners.

• *The unsatisfactory results and complications of unilateral action may be reduced if both partners, before acting, attempt to assess carefully the effects of proposed policies on the other country and to consider alternative ways of achieving a given policy objective.*

All three cases demonstrate that assessment of impacts and consideration of alternatives could have contributed to better outcomes. The NEP exacerbated tensions because Canada failed to take adequate account of how the United States would be affected and how it might react. One hopes that Canada will have learned from this experience when, for example, it faces a decision about exercising the Crown Interest in the Hibernia development. Rather than converting the Crown Interest into a working interest, it could control the pace of development and collect revenues through alternative royalty and regulatory policies that would avoid the U.S. government's concerns about international legal precedents.

The softwood-lumber case illustrates that U.S. trade law has established a system within which Canadian export industries must operate. This system has the advantage of being transparent and relatively free from political influence. But the risk of harassment from import-competing interests remains, as does the possibility that regulatory bodies or the courts will interpret the law in a way that differs from the intentions of U.S. negotiators. Moreover, congressional action to broaden the definition of subsidization in U.S. law could have a negative impact on Canadian resource-management and economic-development policies in the future.

The border-broadcasting case was — and still is — muddied by Canada's failure to clarify whether its policy objective is to support Canadian programing or to ensure the financial viability of Canadian broadcasters. It would also be helpful if Canada could consider alternative ways of meeting these objectives — such as prorated tax deductibility or subsidies from general revenues to programers and broadcasters — that would be more acceptable to U.S. interests.

• *Improved perception of the intentions and concerns of the other government can lessen tensions in the relationship.*

Canadians and Americans alike sometimes misunderstand each other's intentions.[1] Perhaps the best example of the frustration and disillusionment

---

[1] Problems of perception are addressed more generally in Robert Jervis, "Hypotheses on Misperception," *World Politics* 20 (April 1968): 454–479.

that can result from this kind of misperception was the mutually disappointing episode of *ex gratia* payments under the NEP. The Canadian government considered that its substantial flexibility went unappreciated, while the U.S. government considered that promised flexibility had not been forthcoming. The incident was not an isolated example of misperceptions during the NEP dispute; in fact, there was a general tendency by each country to exaggerate the intentions of the other. Mismatched expectations concerning the fluid agenda for negotiations on the NEP also led to problems.

A fundamental difference of perception remains in the border-broadcasting dispute, with lack of agreement on whether the issue should be understood in cultural, economic, or symbolic terms. The Canadian government has failed to understand the strength and tenacity of the U.S. border-broadcasting lobby. Within the United States, the administration and the border broadcasters themselves differ over the desirability of early passage of mirror tax legislation. While the administration's priority is retaliation — to implement reciprocal measures as a symbol of U.S. response to a foreign action — the broadcasters seek a pressure tactic to get Canadian policy changed.

Although sharp differences in Canadian and U.S. interests and objectives are bound to occur, perhaps frequently, these cases suggest that tensions can be reduced if each country were more sensitive to the motives, priorities, and problems of the other. In this way, conflicts can be confined to the substance genuinely at issue, and exaggerated or distorted fears about the other party's intentions can be avoided.

• *Greater sensitivity to the signals one government sends another can make communication clearer, and intentions and priorities better understood.*

Given the modern media, the geographic proximity of Canada and the United States, and the enormous volume of interactions between their residents, rhetoric addressed to one's domestic audience will be heard in the other and can convey signals, intended or unintended, to the other government. Self-congratulatory claims of influence over the actions of the other government intended to impress constituents are likely to have a counterproductive impact on the other side of the border. The rhetoric of confrontation may be appealing to the media, but it is not conducive to compromise. If an issue is publicly characterized in terms of winners and losers, both parties may be unwilling to appear to lose.

The introduction of the NEP was accompanied by much nationalist rhetoric that was directed to a domestic audience but that led many U.S. decisionmakers to exaggerate the intentions of the Canadian government. And the heated response by leading representatives of business, Congress, and the U.S. administration hardened Canadian attitudes on some issues.

Public insensitivity to motives and priorities can strengthen the resolve of the other party to hold firm to principle. Alternatively, being seen to take the other's concerns seriously can make mutually acceptable resolution of a disagreement more likely.

• *A fuller process of consultation between the two governments can create better appreciation in each country of the motives, priorities, and problems of the other and can contribute to a cooperative approach to solving problems.*

Lack of prior consultation or even advance notification about the NEP angered many in the United States, exacerbated tensions, and contributed to many subsequent difficulties. After the fact Canada did consult extensively with the United States, but by then the Canadian public (and members of the Canadian government) were prone to perceive any significant policy changes as bowing to U.S. pressures.

The regular meetings between George Shultz, the U.S. Secretary of State, and Allan MacEachen, the Canadian Secretary of State for External Affairs, were remarkably effective in setting a more positive and relaxed tone for the entire relationship. They resulted in positive developments in preparatory work and in the way government departments and institutions related to each other. The success of these meetings came partly from the good chemistry that stemmed from the pragmatic approach to problem-solving of the two individuals involved. Moreover, Mr. Shultz was prepared to devote time and attention to Canada, a priority that has not always been recognized by his predecessors and may not be by his successors.[2] Yet both a pragmatic approach and a high priority for Canadian-U.S. relations are necessary if ministerial meetings are to make an effective contribution to the relationship.

A number of proposals have been made to extend the process of formal consultation through the creation of new institutions.[3] But this approach may not be the most productive way to improve understanding. The experience of the Joint Canada-United States Committee on Trade and Economic Affairs, for instance, demonstrated that structured consultations can become mechanical or even counterproductive.[4] Both countries tended to store up difficulties for presentation at the meetings rather than dealing with them expeditiously at lower levels. The meetings thus became little more than a cosmetic exercise, an occasion for the recitation of set-piece speeches of little interest to the participants.

[2] It is never difficult to get a Canadian Secretary of State for External Affairs to take a personal interest in relations with the United States.
[3] See Marie-Josée Drouin and Harald B. Malmgren, "Canada, the United States and the World Economy," *Foreign Affairs* 60 (Winter 1981/82): 393–413.
[4] The Joint Canada-United States Committee on Trade and Economic Affairs first met in 1953 and had its last meeting in 1970. The experience of the committee is described in Maureen Appel Molot, "The Role of Institutions in Canada-United States Relations: The Case of North American Financial Ties," in Andrew Axline et al., eds., *Continental Community? Independence and Integration in North America* (Toronto: McClelland and Stewart, 1974), pp. 164–193.

Formalized procedures for fuller consultation may have other drawbacks rooted in the increasing involvement of Congress in Canadian-U.S. relations. Canadian consultations with the U.S. administration can appear to resolve difficulties but still fail if Congress reacts negatively to the agreed-on solutions. Yet consultation with Congress is sometimes not feasible and often inappropriate.

More important, however, are the different impacts that a formal obligation to engage in prior consultation would have on the two governments. Because the United States is so much bigger, it would probably have more impact on Canadian policy than Canada could have on U.S. policy. All things considered, prior consultation on all issues seems unlikely to be acceptable to both parties. Nonetheless, where feasible, prior notification by one country of a new policy and its expected impact on the other could at least focus the debate on factual issues, thus restraining speculation, misperception, and ideological rhetoric.

Another option would be to seek more informal modes of consultation through direct contacts between knowledgeable and aware participants and their counterparts in the other country. Ultimately, as some observers have pointed out, "effective consultation depends far less on machinery and procedure than on the will to consult."[5] It goes without saying that consultation contributes most when the two countries deal with issues on a regular basis, not only when they have become occasions of conflict.

• *Some features of each country's political system can cause genuine problems for the other.*

Marcel Cadieux, a former Canadian ambassador to the United States, once said that the way to improve the bilateral relationship was to change the U.S. constitution.[6] Clearly, Canada does have a problem in that agreements it has negotiated with the U.S. administration may be overturned by Congress. Even executive agreements often require implementing legislation. But these are the constraints of the U.S. political system, and Canada must accept them.

The United States also has problems with the Canadian system, a fact often not recognized by Canadians. The rules of cabinet secrecy, for example, especially in relation to budget measures, represent a serious impediment to outside consultation prior to the official adoption of a policy. Moreover, because Canadian governments are held accountable for their policies, they are often unwilling to make changes once policies have been announced; thus, the potential for subsequent consultation is also limited. (Both problems certainly arose in the case of the NEP.)

---

[5] A.D.P. Heeney and Livingston T. Merchant, *Canada and the United States Principles of Partnership*, [n.p.], June 28, 1965, para. 40.

[6] Quoted in John W. Holmes, *Life with Uncle: The Canadian-American Relationship* (Toronto: University of Toronto Press, 1981), p. 127.

Federal-provincial relationships may also cause problems for the United States because they distract the attention of the Canadian federal government to domestic concerns. In addition, there is always the possibility of uncoordinated policies from eleven governments all having an impact on the United States. These, too, are features of the Canadian constitution that have to be accepted by the United States.

• *Congress's evident and increasing role in Canadian-U.S. relations and its responsiveness to private interests are proving a constraint on bilateral developments.*

As Congress plays an increasingly important role in the bilateral relationship, Canada is likely to rely less on the U.S. administration to relay its interests and concerns to the legislators. Rather, the recent emphasis on public diplomacy, congressional liaison, and lobbying will likely continue to increase. The Canadian government is already learning the benefits of identifying private-sector allies in the United States who will lobby Congress and the U.S. government when their interests coincide with those of Canada. Congress will always be more responsive to domestic pressures than to the pleas of a foreign government that has no vote in the United States. Coalitions with U.S. interests have helped Canada realize its objectives with Congress in several instances, such as the U.S. opposition to the Telidon amendment and the U.S. housing industry's opposition to the imposition of countervailing duties on softwood lumber.

The annual meetings of the Canada-United States Interparliamentary Group, established by joint resolution of the two legislatures, can also be expected to increase in importance.[7] This group can be a forum in which constituency-oriented and possibly parochial members of Congress learn about Canadian interests and concerns from Canadian legislators, who share an awareness of electoral pressures. Simultaneously, members of the Canadian Parliament can become more sensitive to the concerns of U.S. legislators.

Increasing these activities will present some drawbacks to Canada. For instance, if it steps up its lobbying of Congress, U.S. interests may well increase their lobbying activities in Canada. One inevitable result will be attempts to lobby provincial governments directly rather than trying to convince federal legislators of the merits of U.S. positions. (In fact, such contacts with provincial governments have already begun over the NEP and natural-gas exports.) The Canadian government can scarcely argue that it is right and proper for it to intervene directly in the U.S. domestic political process through lobbying, unless the U.S. government is allowed to act in a similar manner in Canada. Another potential problem is that the U.S. administration

---

[7] Matthew J. Abrams, *The Canada-United States Interparliamentary Group* (Ottawa: Parliamentary Centre for Foreign Affairs and Foreign Trade; Toronto: Canadian Institute of International Affairs, 1973).

may resent Canadians' "going behind its back" to deal directly with Congress.

Clearly, direct relations with Congress and the identification of private-sector allies in the United States must be a supplement to, not a replacement for, relations with the U.S. administration. The Canadian government will have to decide when and how various activities should be undertaken, recognizing that one consequence could be increased U.S. lobbying in Canada.

• *Multilateral commitments and dispute-settlement procedures can be an effective means of preventing or resolving bilateral disputes.*

The tensions created by the NEP were effectively eased when the United States took its complaints the multilateral route. Because complaints at this level have to be documented and committee meeting schedules organized, the process is slow and deliberate. This pace in itself can help de-escalate disputes.

The multilateral process offers other benefits, too. For example, the General Agreement on Tariffs and Trade (GATT) panel on Canada's Foreign Investment Review Agency (FIRA) practices provided a more objective basis for examination of the issues and a less-politicized context for resolution of differences than could have been found elsewhere. It was politically more acceptable for Canada to modify its practices in light of the GATT panel finding on FIRA than would have been the case with a bilateral negotiation in which Canada could have been perceived domestically as having succumbed to U.S. pressures.

GATT commitments can also be effective in limiting disputes or preventing them from arising. Before passage of the NEP legislation, the Canadian government amended the procurement provisions to conform with its GATT obligations. In the softwood-lumber case, the GATT agreements had shaped the remedies available to the U.S. producers under their country's trade legislation.

• *Those bilateral issues not covered by multilateral agreements or subject only to broad multilateral statements of principle can cause problems in the bilateral relationship.*

Bilateral differences over the investment issues raised by the NEP have been more persistent than those concerning trade. This is because of differences in the two countries' interpretations of the Organisation for Economic Co-operation and Development (OECD) convention on national treatment. Unlike the GATT commitments, which entail formal obligations and a dispute-settlement process, the OECD declaration is simply a consensus statement of principle. The United States' fundamental concern about the NEP was that it might establish a Canadian and international precedent of derogation from the principle of national treatment. In bilateral meetings with the United States and in the multilateral meetings of the OECD, Canada stated that the NEP was an exception, appropriate to Canadian circumstances, and did not indicate a new trend in Canadian policy. Canada's willingness to comply with multilateral commitments on trade under the GATT contrast with its determination to proceed with an exception to the looser OECD investment guidelines.

Existing multilateral agreements do not cover trade in services. In the absence of such formal arrangements, border broadcasting has become a nagging, persistent problem in Canadian-U.S. relations. A bilateral or multilateral agreement that defines appropriate means of pursuing cultural objectives could help to prevent such disputes from arising in the future and could aid in the resolution of those that do occur.

• *The asymmetry in the Canadian-U.S. economic relationship means that similar policies or legislation can have dissimilar effects in the two countries.*

Canada and the United States have similar legislative provisions and regulatory procedures governing imports. But U.S. trade actions are likely to have much greater impact on Canada than Canadian actions have on the United States. The softwood-lumber case provides an illustration of this asymmetry. The U.S. International Trade Commission's final determination, although favorable to Canada, did label 19 Canadian government programs as conferring subsidies. For products other than lumber, the subsidy finding might well exceed the *de minimis* level. Canadian federal and provincial governments have been given a clear message that they should be careful in designing programs to assist industry since there is a significant risk of U.S. countervail actions against Canadian exports. In contrast, Canadian countervail law is unlikely to constrain or to deter subsidies by U.S. governments.

Better Management of the Relationship

In the years ahead, the Canadian-U.S. relationship will present opportunities for cooperation, but the strains and difficulties must be carefully managed. The most urgent question is how management of the relationship can be improved to avoid costly misunderstandings and to limit irreconcilable differences. Several possibilities exist.

Multilateral Agreements

One way is to rely more heavily on multilateral agreements to harmonize bilateral policy. The existence of such agreements shaped the conduct and resolution of some Canadian-U.S. tensions and disputes during the 1980–83 period, and future emphasis on the linkage between the multilateral framework and the bilateral relationship could benefit both countries. Indeed, the bilateral relationship has functioned best when the two governments have made common cause in multilateral negotiations.

Both countries have an interest in preventing the growth of protectionism that could be served by, for example, collaboration on an international initiative to liberalize trade in services. Such a commitment is already a U.S. policy priority, and further Canadian support would add momentum. A multilateral agreement could contribute to bilateral Canadian policy goals by providing appropriate exemptions for cultural policy measures while opening up markets and forestalling unilateral U.S. actions.

A New Bilateral Approach

Another way of improving the management of the bilateral relationship would be to create a new framework of understanding designed to reduce the injurious effects of unilateral action by either party. Both countries would benefit if they could establish norms to guide their policy actions, particularly in cases for which no multilateral commitment or national legislation applies.[8] If either country could achieve its most-preferred outcome by making independent decisions, there would be no need for such norms and principles. In the Canadian-U.S. relationship, however, outcomes achieved by joint action are often better for both countries than those that are reached independently, so such a framework would be in the interests of both. Another advantage of this informal approach is that it avoids the problem of other countries demanding similar arrangements with the United States.

For many years, the Canadian-U.S. relationship functioned according to a set of implicit rules of conduct that were widely recognized by scholars and policymakers alike. Many of these traditions no longer apply today.[9] In time, a new set of norms and principles or pattern of behavior can be expected to restore more predictability to the way issues are handled in the relationship.[10]

---

[8] The point here is the recent scholarly concept of a "regime", defined as a set of implicit or explicit principles, norms, rules, and procedures around which converge the expectations in a given relationship (see Stephen D. Krasner, ed., *International Regimes*, special issue of *International Organization* 36 [Spring 1982]). It is argued that although regimes may arise spontaneously (like the common law) or may be imposed by some external force (like military conquest), the most interesting are those that are created or changed in response to the self-interest of the parties involved. When two or more countries have a joint interest in avoiding mutually undesired outcomes that would or may result from their separate unilateral action or when joint action offers benefits more satisfying than the suboptimal outcomes attainable from independent unilateral behavior, it is in the self-interest of both countries to accept or create a regime to avoid these dilemmas (see Arthur A. Stein, "Coordination and Collaboration: Regimes in an Anarchic World," *International Organization* 36 [Spring 1982]: 299–324).
[9] See Allan E. Gotlieb, "Canada-U.S. Relations: The Rules of the Game," *SAIS Review* (Summer 1982): 177–187.
[10] The literature on regimes shows that the need and likelihood of a regime is greatest in a situation of great interdependence (see Robert O. Keohane, "The Demand for International Regimes," *International Organization* 36 [Spring 1982]: 325–355). The high level of interdependence between Canada and the United States makes it virtually inevitable that there will be a new bilateral regime of one kind or another.

If each country continues to make unilateral responses to bilateral issues as they arise, some of these emerging standards of conduct may be desirable but others may not. A deliberate attempt to direct their development requires articulation of a new, mutually beneficial relationship. This approach would not mean a return to the old special relationship as such; neither would it represent continental integration, nor the loss of national independence or identity. Rather, it would involve a recognition that when either country acts unilaterally, the outcome can be less than optimal for both partners in the relationship.

Such norms for the conduct of the relationship will only be effective, however, if they are seen to serve the mutual interests of both governments. They could best be developed by consultation among members of the legislative and executive branches of both governments. Such a process would help focus government attention on the identification of common interests. When differences are irreconcilable, a new framework of understanding could help the two countries achieve the best possible outcomes with the least possible negative impacts. When differences are not irreconcilable, the framework could improve the process of reconciliation by avoiding problems and unnecessary tensions.

New guiding principles may, of course, be imprecise, with compliance depending on enlightened self-interest, public commitment, and good faith, rather than on legal sanctions. But this approach might be an advantage. Inflexible rules without a continuing underlying commitment to abide by them are hollow and ineffective. Hard and fast bilateral rules about what must and must not be done may only invite legalistic challenges of interpretation. The more legalistic international arrangements, such as the GATT, appear to work precisely because they are multilateral. In a bilateral relationship, the two parties are unlikely to derive mutual benefit on all issues. Sometimes, particularly when private interests are involved, competition is bound to exist. But both need to consider the long-term mutual benefits that can be achieved by working within publicly accepted principles, even if either could make some short-term gain by unilaterally violating them. While wholly containing the actions of Congress or of the Canadian provinces within predetermined limits may not be possible in all cases, some movement in that direction is possible.

If the new framework is to be widely recognized and respected, governments will have to play a role, not only in developing the principles, but also in giving them formal acceptance. Such endorsement could be made in a variety of ways, ranging from an exchange of memoranda to a summit declaration. Direct involvement of the two federal legislatures in the formulation and development of a framework of understanding would make it more likely that their members would operate within its norms and principles.

Some Principles for a New Framework

Based on the experience of the 1980–83 period, the process of working out a new bilateral framework should include attention to four basic principles:

• *Understanding the motives and priorities of the other government.* Differences are more easily tolerated and the dangers of exaggerated misinterpretation minimized when one government recognizes that the purposes and interests of the other are not necessarily identical to its own and that, therefore, the two countries may not be best served by identical policies. Achieving this understanding requires the fostering in both countries of continuity of senior government personnel who have expertise and breadth of experience and who are willing to give priority to bilateral issues. Ensuring continuity of officials is difficult in the United States because of the turnover in political appointees in senior positions and the career rotation of civil servants. The Canadian-American Committee's proposal that each government structure have a designated focal point with a permanent and experienced staff bears directly on this point, as does the recent re-establishment of the position of U.S. Deputy Assistant Secretary for Canadian Affairs.[11] Similarly, the Canadian government has consolidated the conduct of its economic and political relations with the United States under the jurisdiction of a single assistant deputy minister.

• *Choosing policy instruments that will achieve the desired objective while minimizing the costs imposed on the other country.* Part of each country's policymaking process should be an assessment of the ways in which a proposed policy will affect the other. If that impact is potentially costly, it may be possible to achieve the desired objective by more mutually acceptable means.

• *Developing a fuller process of consultation.* When both parties are receptive, consultation can result in better understanding of the objectives of policy actions and lessen the tensions that result from misperception. Prior consultation on policy changes could help prevent the implementation of measures that might adverse consequences for the other country. Even if a policy is expected to have a negative impact, prior notification of the other partner can forestall an excessive reaction based on fear or misperception and focus the debate on factual issues; it may sometimes lead to discovery of a mutually beneficial or less damaging alternative.

• *Avoiding the linkage of unrelated issues as a coercive tactic.* In an interdependent relationship, so many interests come into play that it can be difficult to distinguish between related and unrelated issues. Moreover, problems can sometimes be resolved by compromises that involve reciprocal concessions. Nevertheless, the deliberate linkage of matters beyond the

---

[11] See Canadian-American Committee, *Improving Bilateral Consultation on Economic Issues*, CAC no. 48 (Washington, D.C.: National Planning Association; Montreal: C.D. Howe Institute, 1981).

bounds of the immediate dispute can often be a confrontationist and escalatory attempt to impose the will of one country on another and is not conducive to a collaborative search for a compromise solution. Private interests will inevitably press for linkage, but both countries will find long-term gain in solutions of mutual benefit, rather than unilateral advantage. Furthermore, the linkage of unrelated issues threatens to violate the principle that the means used in each case should be proportionate to the stakes involved.[12]

Conclusion

Although economic recovery may help to improve relations between Canada and the United States, it will not resolve all problems. Indeed, it could bring new ones. Whatever the government in Ottawa, one must expect continued determination to strengthen the Canadian economy. One must also expect special interests in the United States that do not benefit from the recovery to press Congress to alleviate their relative disadvantage. Continuing changes in the international environment will require both countries to make policy responses that, because of the other underlying factors at play, may well be dissimilar and may create potential sources of conflict.

The bilateral relationship weathered the tempest of the early 1980s. Clouds will continue to appear on the horizon, but the severity of the storms they portend — indeed, whether they might disperse without incident — depends in large part on the capacity of both partners to learn from the past and to alter their conduct so as to achieve greater mutual benefits.

The extraordinary degree of economic interdependence between Canada and the United States means that international pressures, combined with differences between the two countries' decisionmaking processes, policy priorities, and choice of policy instruments are bound to create stresses in the relationship. Yet both countries have an enduring interest in cooperative approaches to these problems. Managing the tensions in bilateral economic relations will require vigilance to identify issues on the horizon, a keen understanding of each other's priorities, and a shared commitment to the cooperative resolution of problems.

---

[12] For example, although the GATT provides for compensation or retaliation in trade disputes, it also has rules circumscribing the extent of the retaliation and requiring that these measures be used only a last resort if negotiations fail.

Members of the
Canadian-American Committee

Cochairmen

STEPHEN C. EYRE
Citicorp Professor of Finance, Pace University, New York, N.Y.

ADAM H. ZIMMERMAN
President and Chief Operating Officer, Noranda Inc., Toronto, Ontario

Vice Chairmen

WILLIAM D. EBERLE
Chairman, EBCO Incorporated, Boston, Massachusetts

J.H. WARREN
Vice Chairman, Bank of Montreal, Montreal, Quebec

Members

JOHN D. ALLAN
Chief Executive Officer, Stelco Inc., Toronto, Ontario

*EDWARD ANDERSEN
Master, National Grange, Washington, D.C.

EDWIN I. ARTZT
President, Procter & Gamble International and Vice Chairman of the Procter & Gamble Company, Cincinnati, Ohio

CHARLES F. BAIRD
Chairman and Chief Executive Officer, INCO Limited, Toronto, Ontario

RALPH M. BARFORD
President, Valleydene Corporation Ltd., Toronto, Ontario

R.R. BAXTER
President, CF Industries, Long Grove, Illinois

ROD J. BILODEAU
Chairman and Chief Executive Officer, Honeywell Limited, Willowdale, Ontario

DAVID I.W. BRAIDE
Vice-Chairman, C-I-L Inc., Toronto, Ontario

PHILIP BRIGGS
Executive Vice-President, Metropolitan Life Insurance Company, New York, N.Y.

KENNETH J. BROWN
President, Graphic Communication International Union, Washington, D.C.

LAWRENCE BURKHART
President, Canadian Kenworth, Ottawa, Ontario

R.W. CAMPBELL
Chairman and Chief Executive Officer, Canadian Pacific Enterprises Ltd., Calgary, Alberta

JOE E. CHENOWETH
Executive Vice-President, International Controls, Honeywell Inc., Minneapolis, Minnesota

W.A. COCHRANE
Chairman and Chief Executive Officer, Connaught Laboratories Limited, Willowdale, Ontario

THOMAS J. CONNORS
Executive Vice-President, Operations, Pfizer International Inc., New York, N.Y.

CHARLES E. CRAIG
Vice-President, International Operations, The Timken Company, Canton, Ohio

MICHAEL V. DAVIES
Vice-President, Internation Operations, The Timken Company, Canton, Ohio

A.J. deGRANDPRE
Chairman, Bell Canada Enterprises Inc., Montreal, Quebec

PETER DeMAY
Group Vice-President, Fluor Engineers Inc., Irvine, California

JOHN H. DICKEY, Q.C.
President, Nova Scotia Pulp Limited, Halifax, Nova Scotia

WILLIAM DIEBOLD, JR.
Upper Nyack, New York

THOMAS W. diZEREGA
Upperville, Virginia

RODNEY S.C. DONALD
Chairman, McLean Budden Limited

CHARLES F. DORAN
Professor and Director, Center of Canadian Studies, Johns Hopkins University School of Advanced International Studies, Washington D.C.

JOHN P. FISHER
Chairman, Fraser Inc., Edmundston, New Brunswick

---

*Became a member after the Statement was circulated for signature.

Committee Members

---

*Became a member after the Statement was circulated for signature.

DOUGLAS R. McNAIR
Vice-President, International Relations, Atlantic-Richfield Company, Los Angeles, California

*JAMES A. MERRILL
Senior Vice President and Chief International Economist, Marine Midland Bank, N.A., New York, N.Y.

JOHN MILLER
Vice Chairman, National Planning Association, Washington, D.C.

FRANK J. MORGAN
President and Chief Operating Officer, The Quaker Oats Company, Chicago, Illinois

HARRY E. MORGAN, JR.
Senior Consultant, Weyerhaeuser Company, Tacoma, Washington

FRANK E. MOSIER
Senior Vice-President, Standard Oil Company of Ohio, Cleveland, Ohio

J.D. MUNCASTER
President and Chief Executive Officer, Canadian Tire Corporation Ltd., Toronto, Ontario

J.J. MUNRO
President, Western Canadian Regional Council No. 1, International Woodworkers of America, Vancouver, B.C.

RICHARD W. MUZZY
Executive Vice-President, Owens-Corning Fiberglas Corporation, Toledo, Ohio

MILAN NASTICH
President, Ontario Hydro, Toronto, Ontario

OWEN J. NEWLIN
Vice-President, Pioneer Hi-Bred International Inc. Des Moines, Iowa

JAMES R. NININGER
President, The Conference Board of Canada, Ottawa, Ontario

CHARLES A. PERLIK, JR.
President, The Newspaper Guild (AFL-CIO, CLC), Washington, D.C.

CHARLES PERRAULT
President, Perconsult Ltd., Montreal, Quebec

GEORGE J. POULIN
General Vice-President, International Association of Machinists & Aerospace Workers, Washington, D.C.

LAWRENCE G. RAWL
Director and Senior Vice-President, Exxon Corporation, New York, N.Y.

A.E. SAFARIAN
Department of Economics, University of Toronto, Toronto, Ontario

JAMES R. SCHLESINGER
Senior Advisor, Lehman Brothers, Shearson Lehman/American Express Inc., New York, N.Y.

J.M.G. SCOTT
Vice Chairman, Wood Gundy Inc., Toronto, Ontario

C. RICHARD SHARPE
Chairman and Chief Executive Officer, Sears Canada Inc., Toronto, Ontario

JACK SHEINKMAN
Secretary-Treasurer, Amalgamated Clothing and Textile Workers' Union, New York, N.Y.

RAY V. SMITH
President and Chief Executive Officer, MacMillan Bloedel Limited, Vancouver, B.C.

DWIGHT D. TAYLOR
Senior Vice-President, Crown Zellerbach Corporation San Francisco, California

KENNETH TAYLOR
Senior Vice-President, Government Affairs, Nabisco Brands, Inc., New York, N.Y.

ROBERT C. THOMAS
President, Tennessee Gas Transmission, Houston, Texas

W. BRUCE THOMAS
Vice Chairman-Administration & Chief Financial Officer, United States Steel Corp., Pittsburg, Pennsylvania

T.H. THOMSON
Senior Vice-President, Imperial Oil Ltd., Toronto, Ontario

ALEXANDER C. TOMLINSON
President, National Planning Association, Washington, D.C.

PETER M. TOWE
Chairman, Petro-Canada International Assistance Corporation, Ottawa, Ontario

F.H. TYAACK
President and Chief Executive Officer, Westinghouse Canada Inc., Toronto, Ontario

R.D. WENDEBORN
Executive Vice-President, Ingersoll-Rand Company, Woodcliff Lake, New Jersey

JOHN R. WHITE
New York, N.Y.

P.N.T. WIDDRINGTON
President and Chief Executive Officer, John Labatt Limited, London, Ontario

WILLIAM P. WILDER
Chairman of the Board, The Consumers' Gas Company Ltd., Toronto, Ontario

LYNN R. WILSON
President, United Steelworkers of America, Pittsburgh, Pennsylvania

LYNTON R. WILSON
President and Chief Executive Officer, Redpath Industries Limited, Toronto, Ontario

FRANCIS G. WINSPEAR
Edmonton, Alberta

GEORGE W. WOODS
Vice-Chairman, TransCanada PipeLines Limited, Toronto, Ontario

*Became a member after the Statement was circulated for signature.

Committee Members

CHARLES WOOTTON
Director, International Public Affairs, Gulf Oil
Corporation, Pittsburgh, Pennslyvania

HAL E. WYATT
Vice-Chairman, The Royal Bank of Canada, Calgary,
Alberta

J.O. WRIGHT
Secretary, Canadian Co-Operative Wheat Producers
Limited, Regina, Saskatchewan

Honorary Members

THOMAS E. COVEL
Marion, Massachusetts

WILLIAM DODGE
Ottawa, Ontario

M.W. MACKENZIE
Ottawa, Ontario

HON. N.A.M. MacKENZIE
Vancouver, B.C.

JOHN R. WHITE
New York, N.Y.

Selected Publications of the Canadian-American Committee*

*These and other Committee publications may be ordered from the Committee's offices at Glendon Hall, 2275 Bayview Avenue, Toronto, Ontario M4N 3M6, and at 1616 P Street, N.W., Washington, D.C. 20036. Quantity discounts are given.